LOS ANGELES

THEN AND NOW®

ACKNOWLEDGMENTS
To Richard Adkins of History For Hire and Christy McAvoy of
Hollywood Heritage. Special thanks to Gayle Bartos Pool for
her guidance. And most of all—to the memory of my late
husband Rick Cameron, my inspiration always.
.
PICTURE CREDITS
The publisher wishes to thank the following for kindly
supplying the "then" photography for this book:
Pages 8, 12, 22, 24, 34, 39 and 88 courtesy of the Library of
Congress.
Pages 16, 26, 30, 36, 46, 48, 66 and 90 courtesy of the
California Historical Society, Title Insurance and Trust Photo
Collection, Department of Special Collections, University of
Southern California.
Pages 10, 18, 20, 32, 44, 70, 86, and 92 courtesy of Getty
Images.
Page 14 courtesy of the Whittington Collection, Department of
Special Collections, University of Southern California.
Page 38, courtesy of the Hearst Newspaper Collection, Special
Collections, University of Southern California.
Pages 28, 44, 50, 62, 64, 74, 76, 78, 80, 82, 84 and 94 courtesy of
the Los Angeles Public Library.
Pages 52, 54, 58, 60, 66, 68 and 72 courtesy of the Bruce
Torrence Hollywood Historical Collection.
Page 40 Courtesy of Alamy.

All "now" images courtesy of Karl Mondon/Pavilion Image
Library.

LOS ANGELES
THEN AND NOW®

ROSEMARY LORD

PAVILION

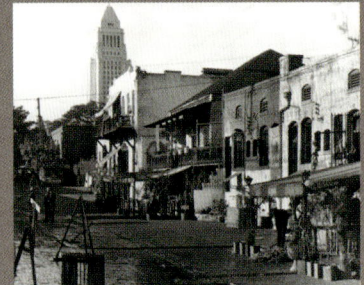

Olvera Street, c. 1940 p. 10

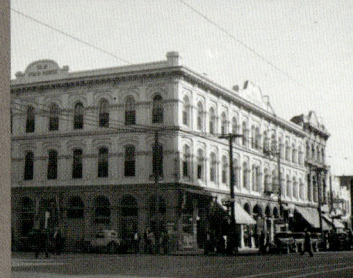

Pico House, 1936 p. 12

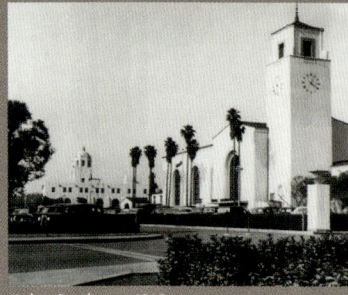

Union Station, c. 1940 p. 16

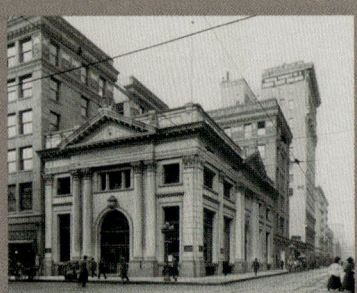

Farmers and Merchants Bank, 1908 p. 24

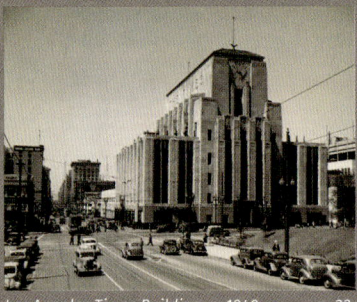

Los Angeles Times Building, c. 1940 p. 32

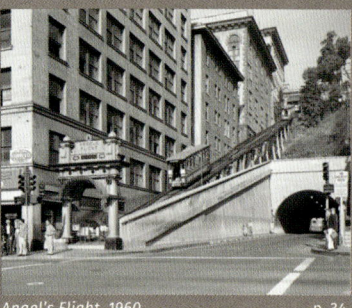

Angel's Flight, 1960 p. 34

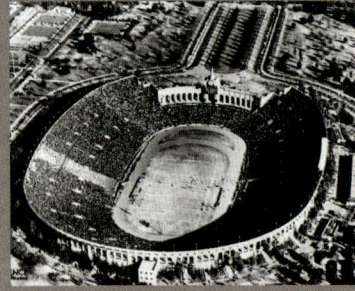

Los Angeles Coliseum, c. 1935 p. 42

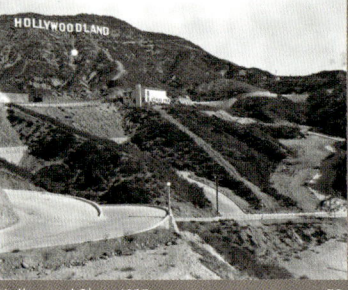

Hollywood Sign, 1935 p. 50

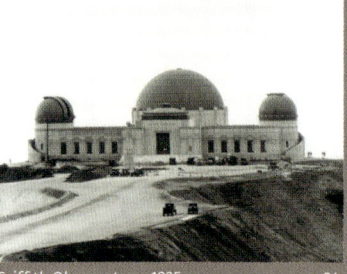

Griffith Observatory, 1935 p. 54

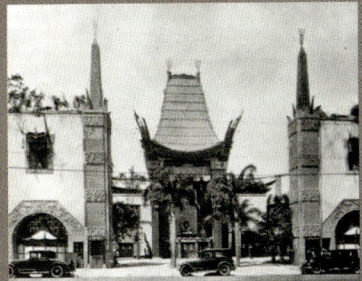
Grauman's Chinese Theatre, c. 1925   p. 62

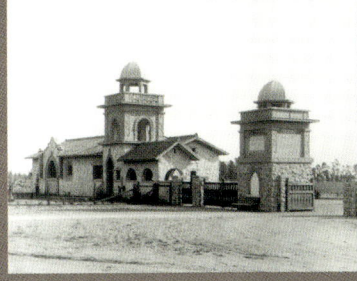
Hollywood Memorial Park, c. 1910   p. 68

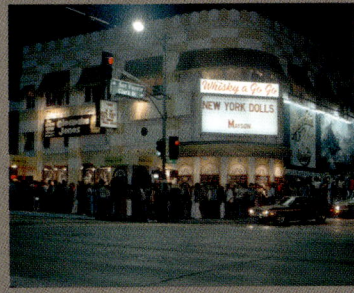
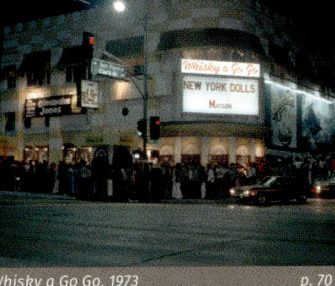
Whisky a Go Go, 1973   p. 70

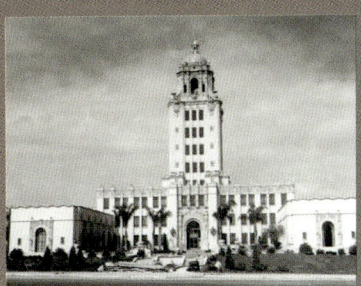
Beverly Hills City Hall, c. 1931   p. 76

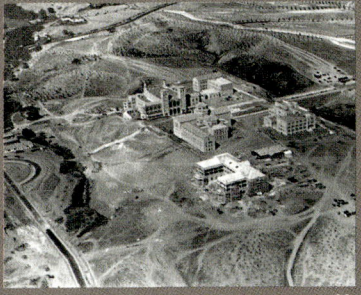
UCLA, 1929   p. 80

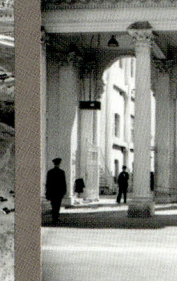

MGM-Sony Studios, c. 1925   p. 82

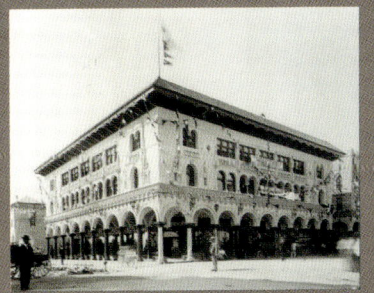
St. Mark's Hotel, c. 1905   p. 88

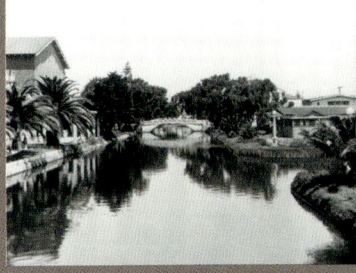
Venice Canal, c. 1935   p. 90

Santa Monica Pier, c. 1940   p. 94

LOS ANGELES

THEN AND NOW INTRODUCTION

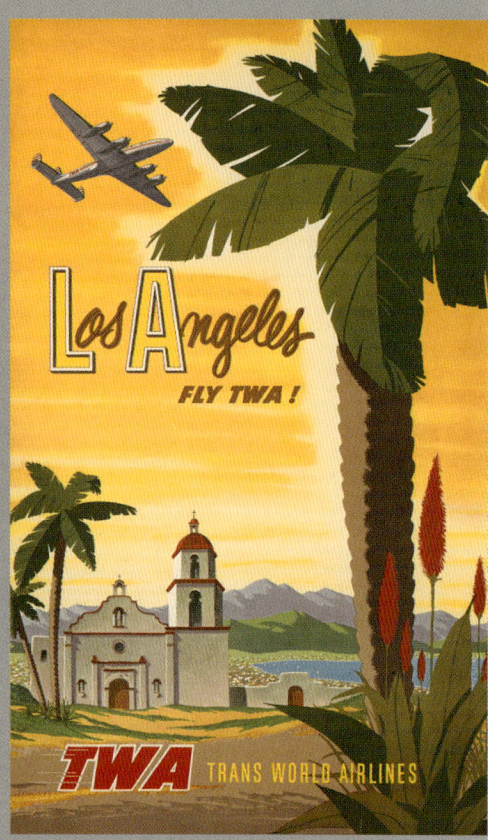

The Native Americans called Los Angeles "the Land of Smoke" because of the haze that often hangs over the basin early in the morning. They were the first to inhabit the area that is now downtown Los Angeles, which they called Yang-Na. In 1542, when Portuguese-born explorer Juan Cabrillo sailed into the harbor, he saw the smoke from the Native Americans' fires and called it "the Bay of Smokes." The early morning haze still lingers, but Los Angeles has continued to change over the decades, probably more than any other part of America.

For years, Los Angeles was just a stopping-off point between Europe and the Far East for traders of spices and silks. It was not until the Spanish, under Gaspar de Portolá's command, arrived at Yang-Na in 1769 that it was claimed and dedicated as "La Reina des los Angeles." The Spanish governor, Felipe de Neve, brought recruits from Mexico, and the forty-four settlers (which included Africans, Native Americans, Spaniards, and Mexicans) officially founded Los Angeles in 1781. Franciscan friar Junípero Serra built missions in an attempt to convert the resident Native Americans to the Christian faith.

The Native Americans were skilled craftspeople, and were used as slave labor to build the new town. In 1860 the Native American population was decimated by an outbreak of smallpox, and by 1920 only five percent of the original Native American population had survived. Unlike the fossilized remains of prehistoric animals trapped in La Brea tar pits, there are scant traces of the Chumash and Tongva tribes, save a few woven baskets, stone paintings, and place-names such as Malibu, Cahuenga, and Azusa.

The first American in Los Angeles was Boston shipbuilder Joseph "Pirate Joe" Chapman in 1818. A gifted carpenter, he built the Pueblo Plaza Church. As the town spread, enterprising developers advertised: "Room for millions of immigrants, a climate for health and wealth with no cyclones or blizzards." Los Angeles was on its way to becoming a polyglot of nations. The Chinese arrived in 1870 to work as cheap labor in the gold mines and on the railroads. The gold rush also brought folks from far and wide in search of their fortunes. Many immigrants, fleeing religious persecution in Europe, came to New York and from there they made the long overland trek west in covered wagons, searching for freedom and sunshine. The majority of Los Angelenos were born elsewhere—even the palm trees that are so widespread in the area (and featured in TWA's glamorous travel poster campaigns of the 1950s, see left) are not indigenous to the region.

The arrival of Henry Huntingdon's Pacific Electric Railroad in 1900 marked the beginning of the trolley system that linked downtown with the ocean and midtown with the valley. In 1851 the *Los Angeles Star* was the town's first newspaper, while the rival *Los Angeles Times* was founded in 1881. Libraries, museums, schools, and places of worship sprang up. Oil was discovered, and the cattle ranchers prospered on this "black gold."

Hollywood was created by Kansas prohibitionist Harvey Wilcox, who sold parcels of his ranch for a development to be called Figwood. However, Wilcox's wife Daeida liked the name Hollywood (a city near Chicago), and the name stuck. Little did the puritanical couple know how their innocent-sounding name would be viewed a century later. It was the Hollywood film industry that really put Los Angeles on the map, as the world escaped into their celluloid adventures and followed the often scandalous and extravagant lifestyles of the movie stars.

In 1909 bad weather in Chicago forced director Francis Boggs to complete his film in Los Angeles. *The Heart of a Race Tout* was shot in a vacant downtown Chinese laundry. However, it was New Yorkers Carl Laemmle, Cecil B. DeMille, Jesse Lasky, and Samuel Goldwyn who first

built movie studios in Hollywood. DeMille's *Squaw Man* became the first feature to be filmed entirely in Hollywood. The legendary Louis B. Mayer, Jack Warner, David Selznick, and showman Sid Grauman continued the legacy, and soon the Hollywoodland sign symbolized the heart of the movie industry. Hollywood gave us films like *Gone With the Wind*, *The Grapes of Wrath*, and *It's a Wonderful Life*, and continues to entertain us today, whether via the cinema or through the broad story arcs of television series.

Today, foreign corporations own most of the film studios, and young hopefuls still flock to seek fame and fortune in Hollywood. A small train stop called Morocco became the elegant Beverly Hills area, which contains Rodeo Drive, a shopping mecca for designer fashions. The swinging 1960s saw an effort to wipe out the old and "modernize," and many beautiful buildings were torn down. Fortunately, today there is a new appreciation of the history of the "Queen of the Angels," and historical societies are busy reclaiming and restoring the old buildings.

Surviving disastrous flooding, fires, riots, and, of course, earthquakes, Los Angeles continues to attract new residents and visitors alike. This revealing book matches historic nineteenth and early twentieth century images with photographs of modern Los Angeles, showing how the multifaceted, multicultural "Dream City" has evolved while retaining its appeal as a place where dreams are realized.

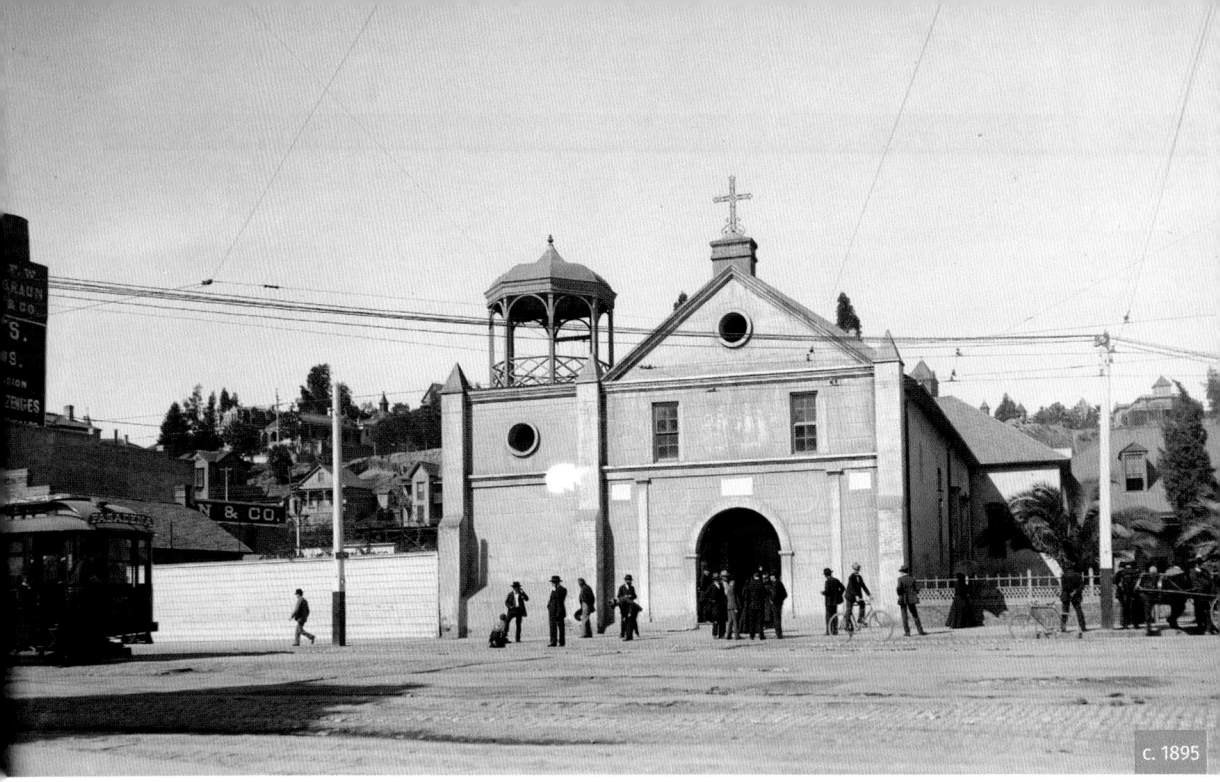

c. 1895

OLD PLAZA CHURCH

The church is still thriving after work on it began over 200 years ago

ABOVE: Shipbuilder Joseph Chapman took four years to build Nuestra Señora la Reina de Los Angeles—Our Lady Queen of the Angels—the first church in Los Angeles, which was dedicated in 1822. The cornerstone was laid in 1814 in what was then the ruins of a small adobe mission. Until then, the Mission San Gabriel was the nearest place of worship for parishioners who walked the nine miles for Sunday services and holy days. The new church quickly became the spiritual and social center for the pueblo. The archive photo is by William Henry Jackson; it was taken between 1890 and 1900 and shows the church after it was rebuilt in 1861.

8

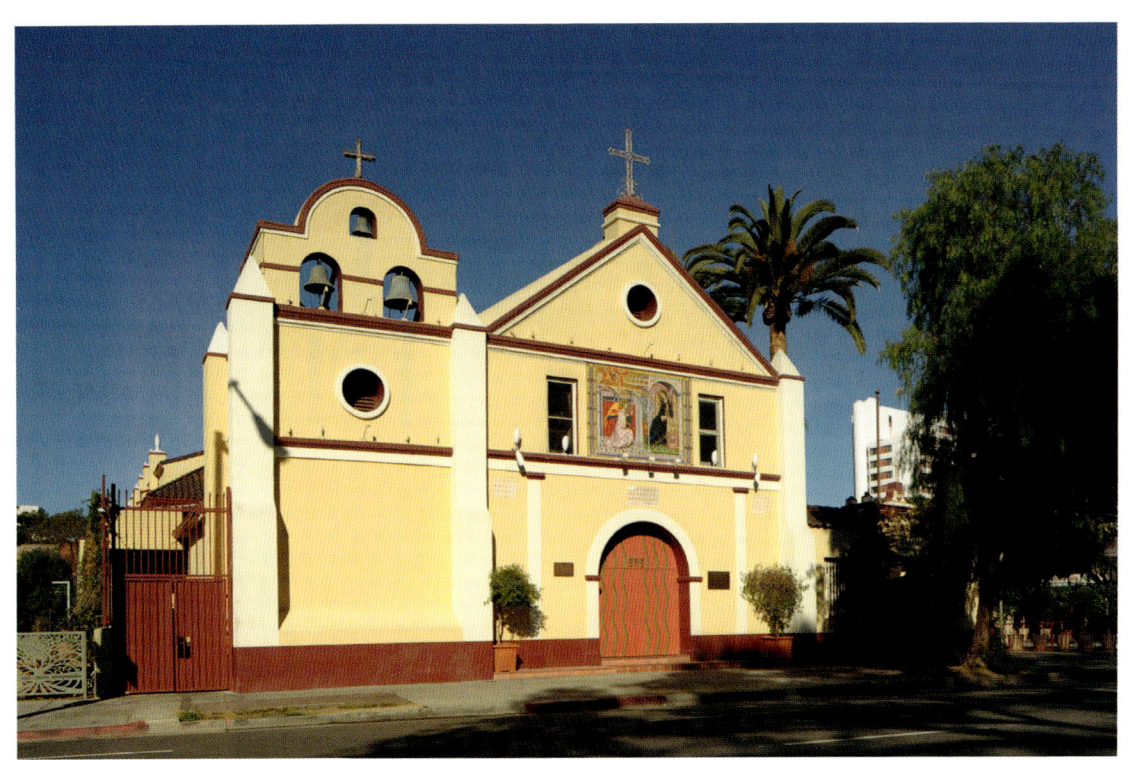

ABOVE: The church has been run by the Claretian Missionary Fathers since 1908 and maintains a strong role in the community. It was one of the first three Los Angeles Historic-Cultural Monuments nominated in 1962, and in the 1980s it gave sanctuary to refugees from El Salvador who had been threatened with deportation. Sparkling with fresh paint, the church is still popular for weddings, christenings, and fiestas. Once boasting the largest Roman Catholic congregation west of the Rockies, the doors are still open to immigrants and refugees in need. Over the years, the Old Plaza Church has had several facelifts—and retrofits—but the church's role remains the same as it watches over the plaza.

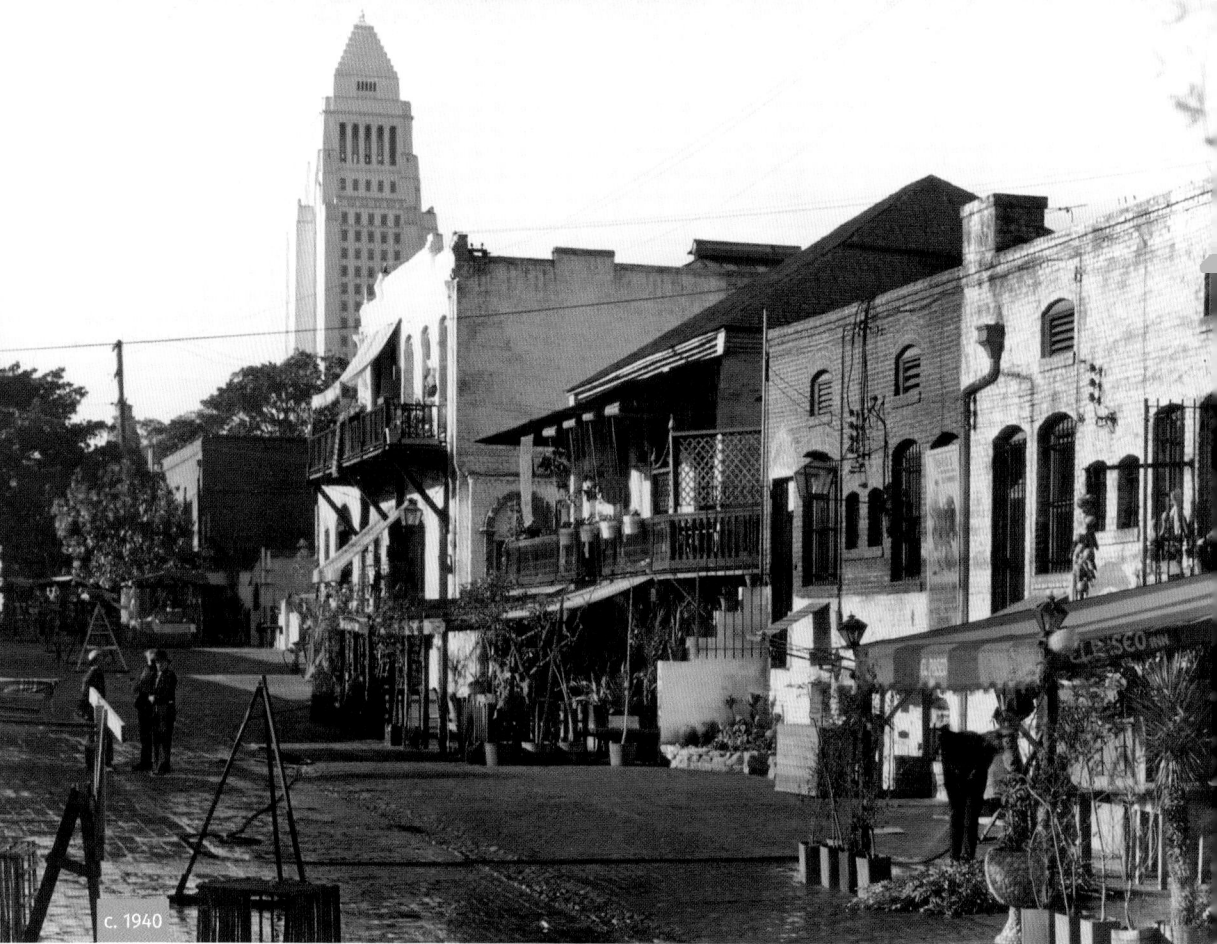

c. 1940

OLVERA STREET
The oldest street in Los Angeles

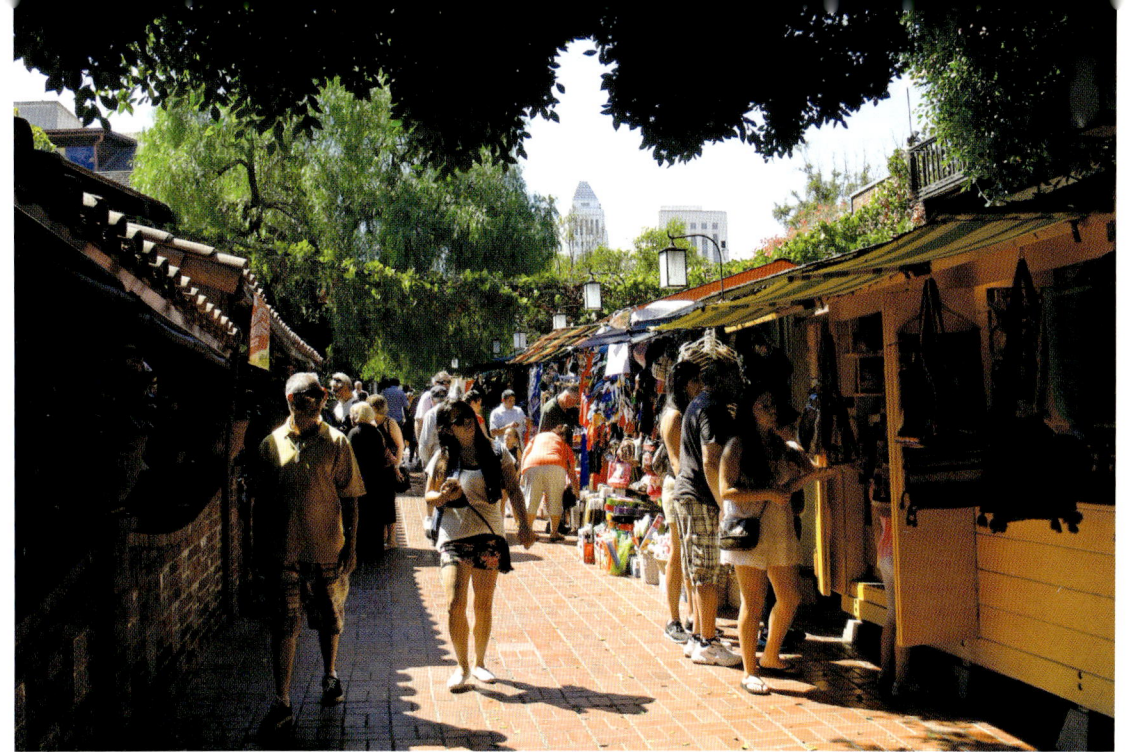

LEFT: Considered the oldest street in Los Angeles, Olvera Street began as a lane called Wine Street on the north side of the plaza. In 1877 it was renamed in honor of one of its residents, Agustin Olvera, the county's first judge. However, by the 1920s the historical buildings were neglected and Olvera Street was in disrepair. In 1926 civic leader Christine Sterling, shocked to find it now a slum, began a campaign to renovate Olvera Street, enlisting her wealthy and influential friends to save this historic heart of Los Angeles.

ABOVE: On Easter Sunday 1930, Olvera Street (paved in bricks by a local prison gang) reopened as a Mexican marketplace, and became an immediate tourist attraction. Of the four original Italian structures on the street, the Winery and the 1857 Pelanconi house remain. In 1930 the latter became La Golondrina and is the oldest restaurant in the area, while the 1818 Avila adobe (Sterling's home until her death in 1963) is the oldest existing building in the city. Today this is an exciting tourist and cultural draw with Mexican artifacts, museums, crafts, restaurants, mariachis, and Aztec dancers to entertain visitors.

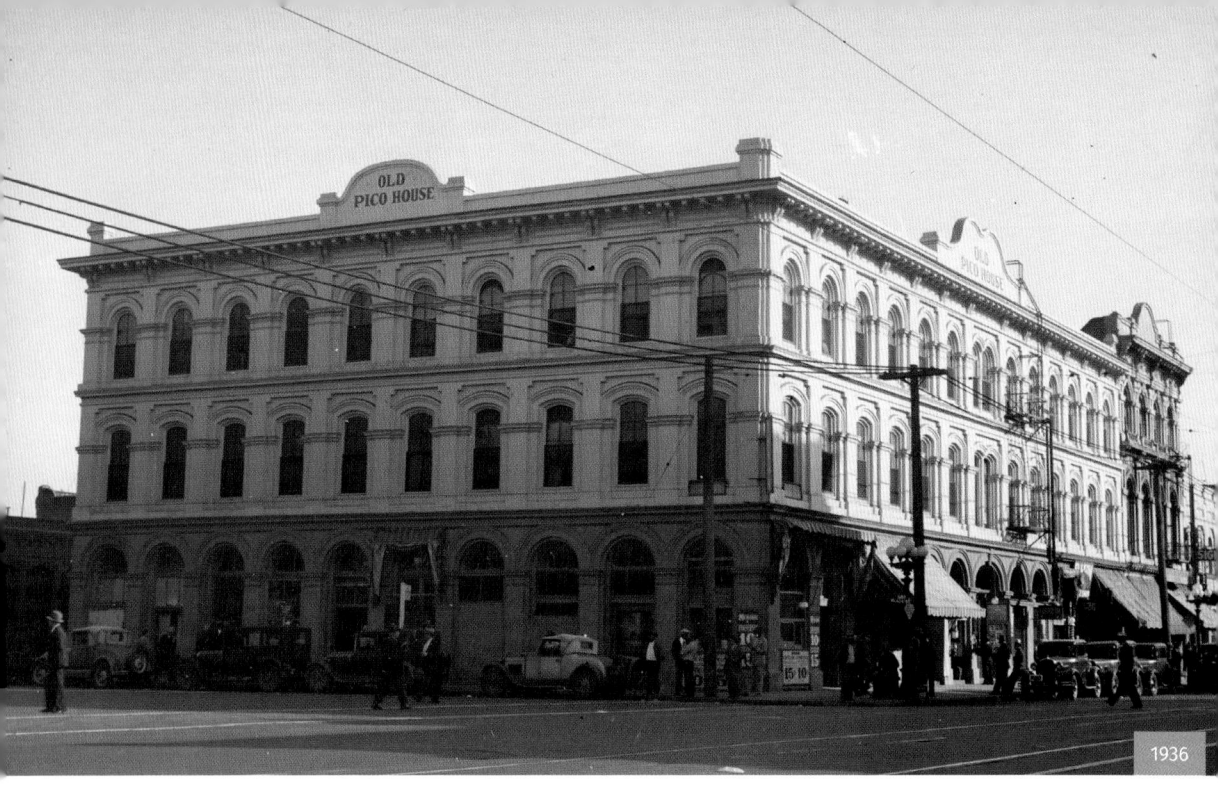

1936

PICO HOUSE

While the Pueblo Plaza was the hub of Los Angeles business, the Pico did a roaring trade

ABOVE: In 1869 Pío Pico, the last Mexican governor of Alta California, built the Italianate Pico House in an effort to revitalize the deteriorating Pueblo Plaza. The first three-story structure there, the Pico House was an elegant hotel with luxurious baths, gas lighting, and a French restaurant. It was designed by Ezra F. Kysor, who also designed the Cathedral of St. Vibiana. Distinguished guests attended balls, wedding receptions, and fiestas. For several years the Pico House was the grandest hotel in Los Angeles—until the business hub of the new city began to move south and the Pueblo Plaza fell into decline at the turn of the twentieth century.

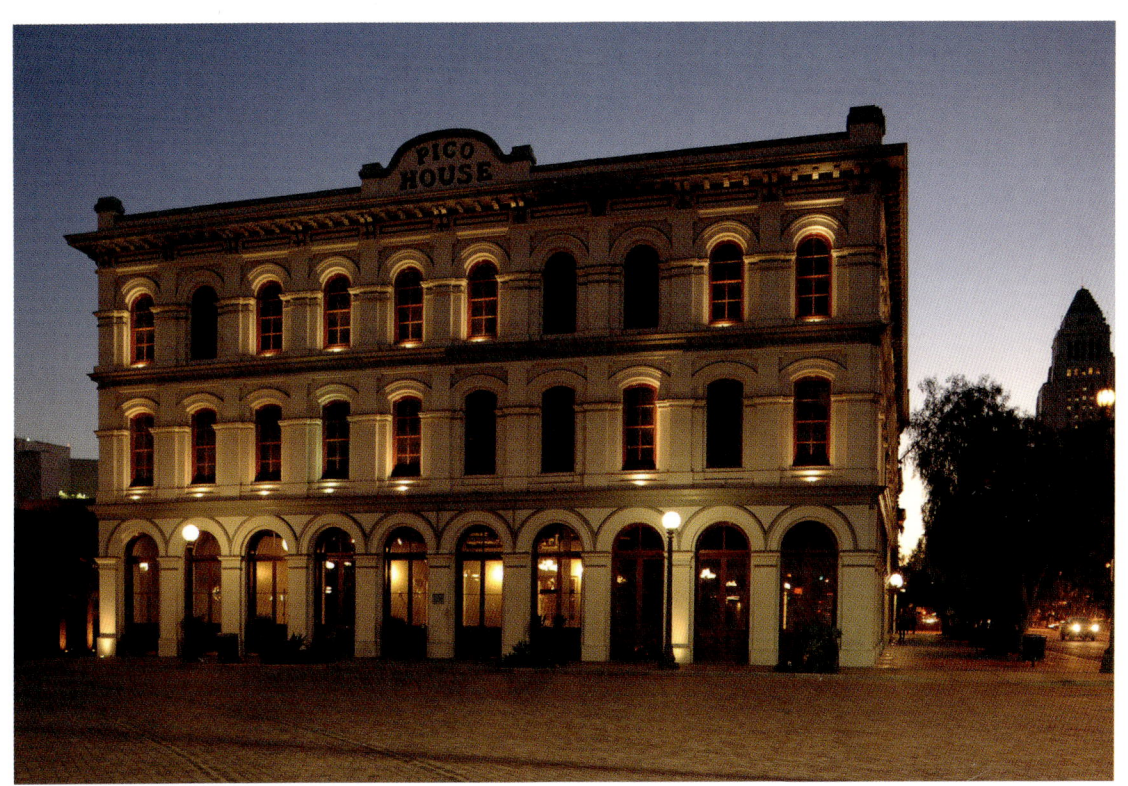

ABOVE: Floods and droughts caused many ranchers to move away from El Pueblo. The Pico House and the adjacent Merced Theatre were successful for a while, but they eventually declined along with the rest of the area. It finally passed into the hands of the State of California in 1953, and it now belongs to the El Pueblo de Los Angeles State Historic Monument. The Pico House was partially renovated in 1981 and again in 1992. After yet another careful restoration, the Pico House now hosts art and photography exhibitions, music recitals, and cultural and social events. The Pico House is frequently used as a site for films, television shows, and commercials.

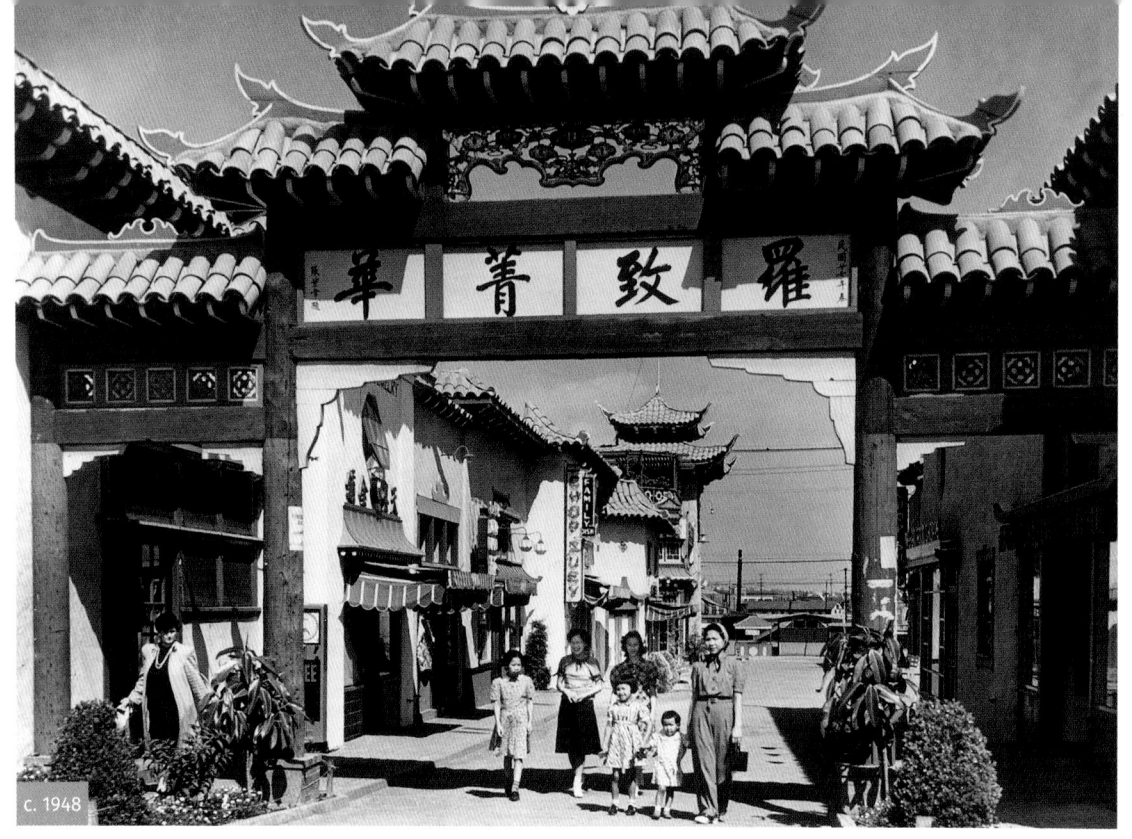

c. 1948

CHINATOWN
Moved from its original location

ABOVE: By 1870 about 300 Chinese people were living in Old Chinatown, south of the plaza, in rundown conditions, plagued with Tong wars, prostitution, and opium dens. The Chinese tenants were unceremoniously evicted from this area in 1932, as the land was to be used for the new Union Station. Not permitted to live among the general population, Chinese residents were moved en masse to share Little Italy a few blocks west.

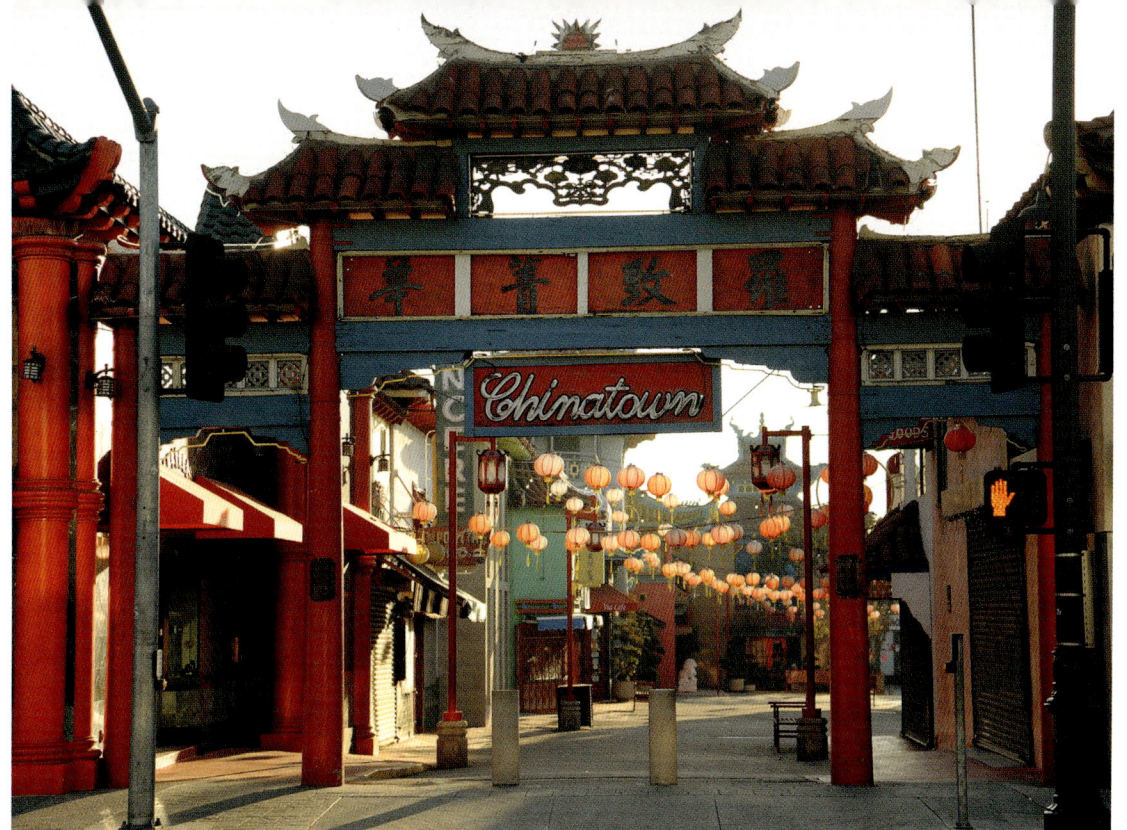

ABOVE: The first "China City"—designed by American filmmakers who filmed scenes for *The Good Earth* (1937)—mysteriously burned down six months later. The new Chinatown, seen today between Broadway and Hill Street, was built in the 1930s on Chinese-owned land, with Chinese input, to provide modern amenities and comfort while retaining Chinese traditions. Chinatown quickly became a favorite with Los Angelenos and tourists alike.

Served by the Gold Line of L.A.'s Metro Rail, Chinatown celebrates the Chinese New Year with the annual Golden Dragon Parade. The dozens of floats, entertainers, and marching bands attract thousands of viewers in the Asian American community. The mid-autumn Lunar Festival and the Firecracker 5K run are popular local events. Films and television shows that have been shot here include *Lethal Weapon*, *Rush Hour,* and (not surprisingly) *Chinatown*.

UNION STATION

Back from the brink, Union Station bustles again in the new century

BELOW: A civic gala opened Union Station in 1939 on Alameda Street (the former site of Old Chinatown), opposite the plaza. It served the Southern Pacific, Santa Fe, and Union Pacific railroads, and was designed by John and Donald Parkinson in a Spanish Mission style with carved ceilings, marbled floor, and a 135-foot clock tower. Before air travel became widespread, Union Station was the arrival and departure point for all Los Angelenos, including wartime GIs and movie stars such as Greta Garbo and Cary Grant.

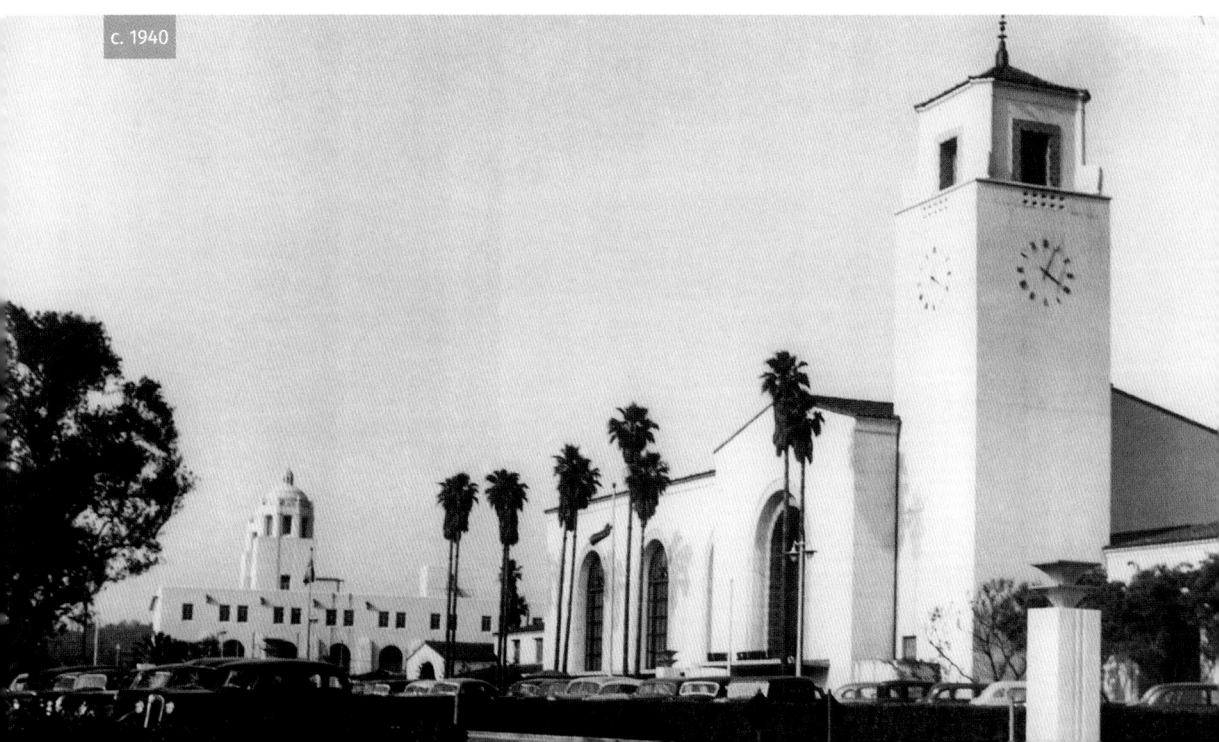

c. 1940

BELOW: Considered the last of America's great railway stations to be built, Union Station fell on hard times when air travel became popular in the 1970s. The 1990s saw a resurgence at Union Station when the Metro Line Subway Terminal opened. Amtrak's Coastal Starlight and San Diegan emerged as the new favorite way to travel and the station's Traxx restaurant the place to eat. In 2011 the L.A. Metropolitan Transportation Authority bought Union Station for $75 million. They added several retail and dining businesses to the concourse and, in September 2013, opened the Metropolitan Lounge for business travelers. A favorite location for film and television companies, with over sixty filming sessions a year, this distinctive setting can be seen in many films, including *The Way We Were*, *Blade Runner*, and *The Dark Knight Rises*.

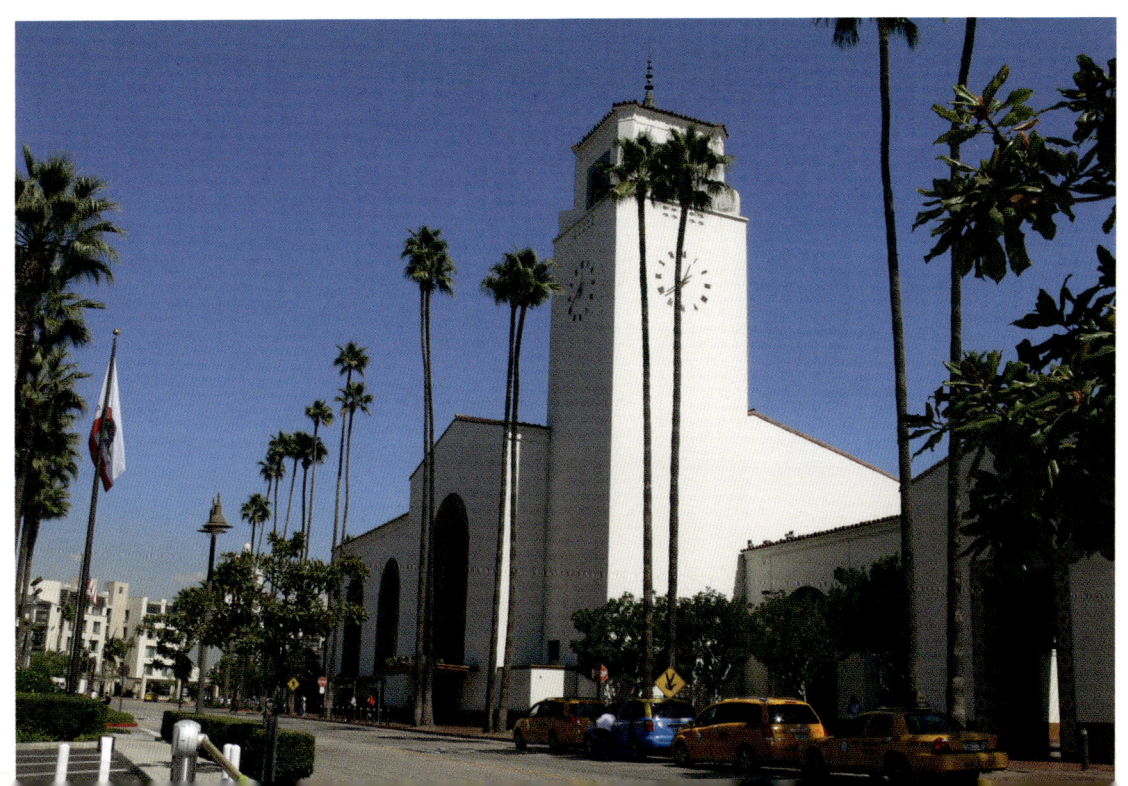

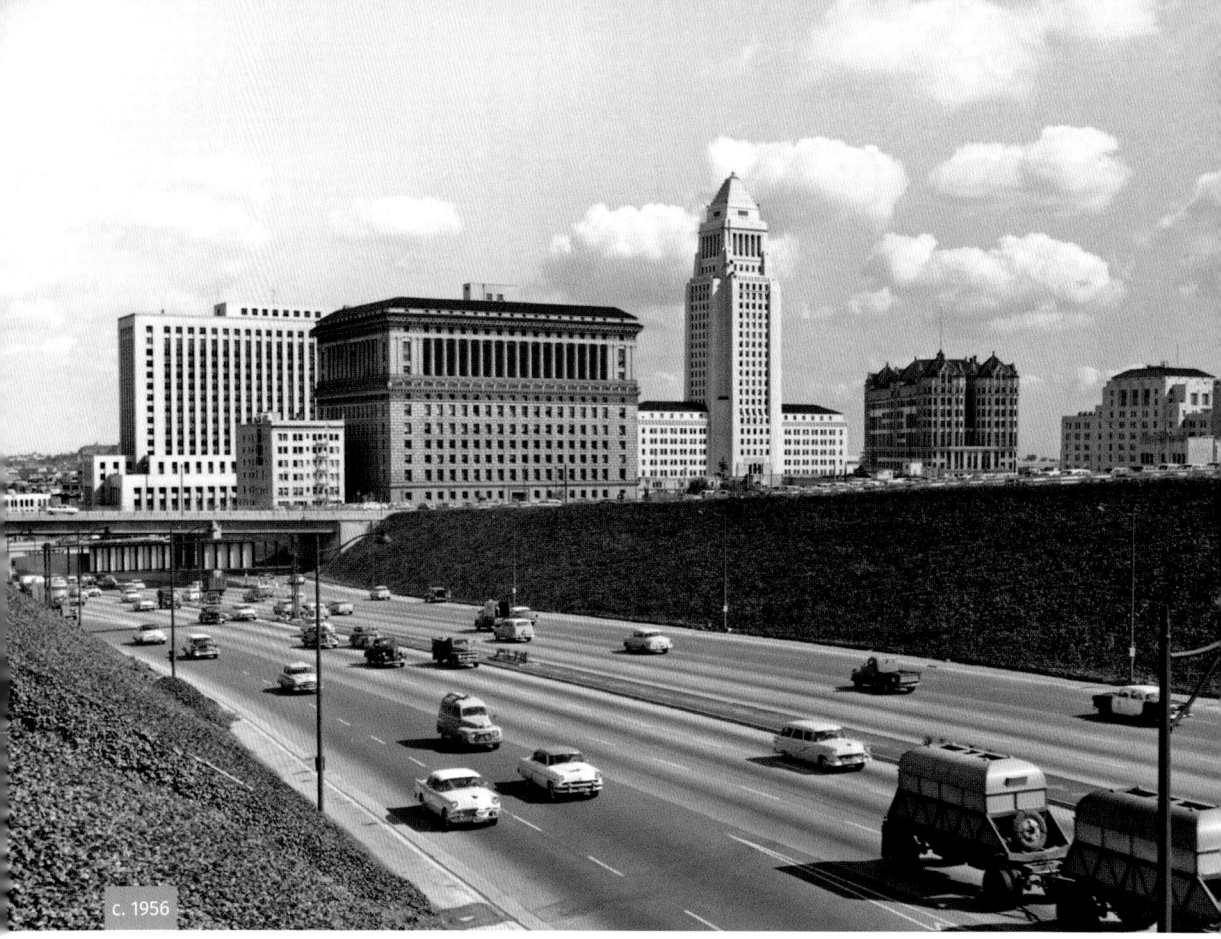

c. 1956

HOLLYWOOD FREEWAY

The route opened up development of the San Fernando Valley

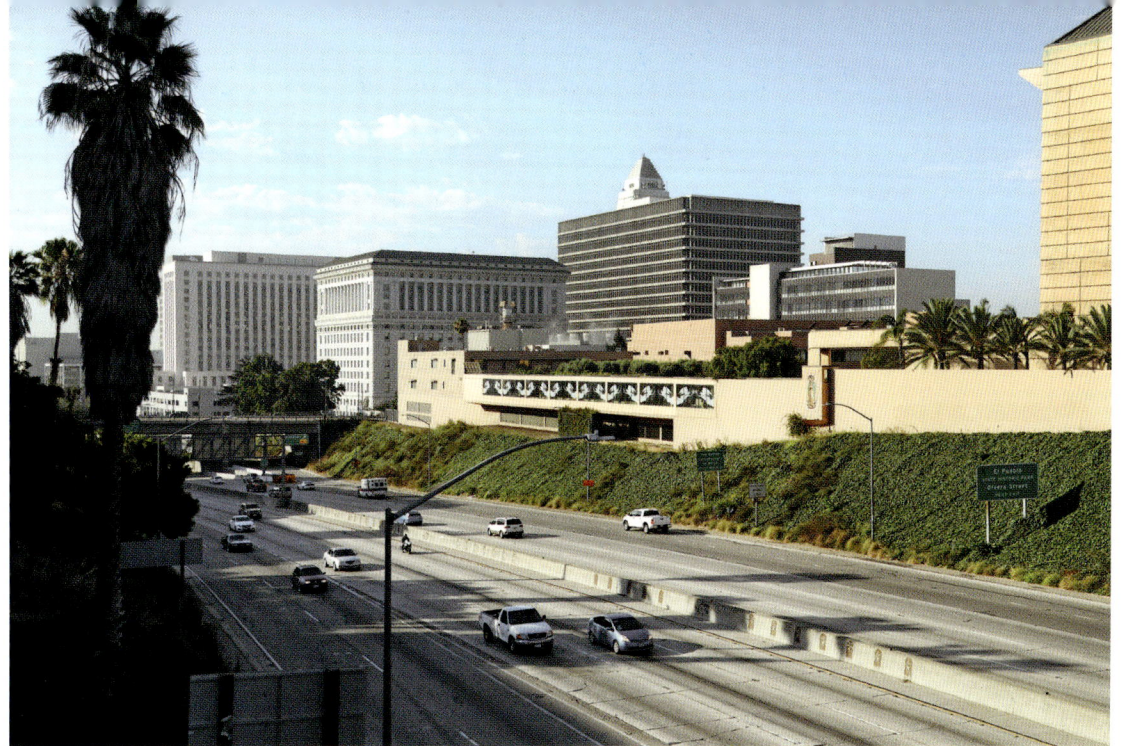

LEFT: The Hollywood Freeway may only be the second oldest in Los Angeles (after the Arroyo Seco Parkway) but it is arguably the most important. It was planned as early as 1924, but the first segment didn't get the ribbon cut until 1940. It was originally called the Cahuenga Pass Freeway and was designed to have trolleys running down a central median. By 1952 the trolleys had gone and two years later the section linking San Fernando Valley to Los Angeles was opened. Seen here around 1956 with traffic flowing freely, traffic congestion soon built up. Comedian Bob Hope called it the most expensive parking lot in the world.

ABOVE: Many historic properties were demolished to make way for Los Angeles's prestigious new highway, including Rudolf Valentino's former home in Whitley Heights. It now forms part of the 101 Freeway which runs along the west coast from downtown Los Angeles through the San Francisco Bay area, Oregon, and ends in Washington state One of the more bizarre stories attached to it is that of the Hollywood Freeway Chickens, a colony of feral chickens that live around the Vineland Avenue off-ramp. The original chickens supposedly escaped when a poultry truck overturned at the junction around 1970.

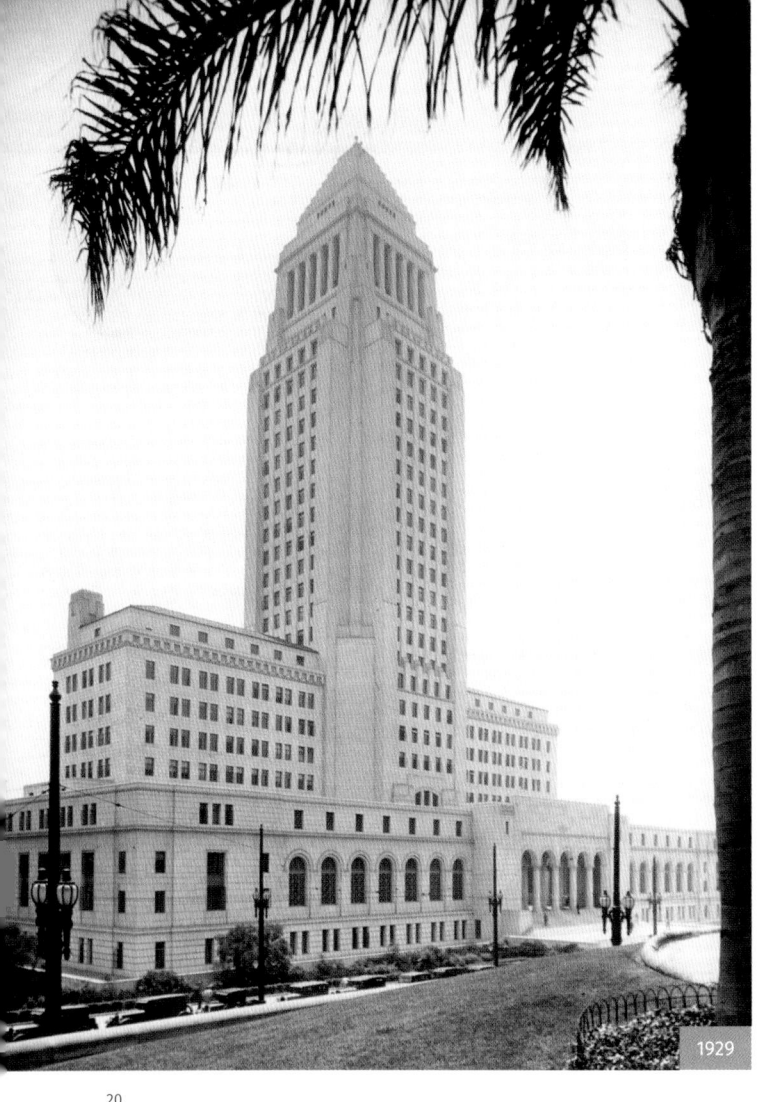

1929

CITY HALL

The iconic building that made it onto LAPD badges

LEFT: City Hall began scraping the sky just as the 1920s were coming to an end. Architects John Parkinson, John C. Austin, and Albert C. Martin Sr. designed the thirty-two-story building that, at 454 feet, stood as the tallest building in Los Angeles until 1968, when the 514-foot Union Bank Building rose up. The building is Los Angeles's third city hall building. The first, the Rocha House, stood on the northeast corner of Spring and Court Streets; the second, a grand Romanesque Revival affair, stood on Broadway between Second and Third Streets. Builders fashioned the concrete in its tower using sand from each of California's fifty-eight counties and water from the state's twenty-one historical missions. An image of City Hall has graced the Los Angeles Police Department's badges since 1940 and became a television icon when Joe Friday (played by Jack Webb) kept the city free of crime in the 1950s on the television series *Dragnet*.

RIGHT: City Hall boasts an observation level open to the public, on the twenty-seventh floor. The Metro Red Line's Civic Center Station serves City Hall and the adjacent federal, state, and county buildings. The 1971 Sylmar earthquake, the 1987 Whittier earthquake, and the 1994 Northridge earthquake all damaged City Hall to varying degrees. Between 1998 and 2001, the building underwent a seismic retrofit that should allow it to sustain minimal damage and remain functional in the event of a magnitude 8.2 earthquake. Making the building as safe as possible is nothing new. The building's original architects separated each floor with flexible compression zones that mimic the human spine in their ability to twist, shake, and return to their original form. Government functions have grown over the years to necessitate the building of a sixteen-story City Hall East and an eight-story City Hall South.

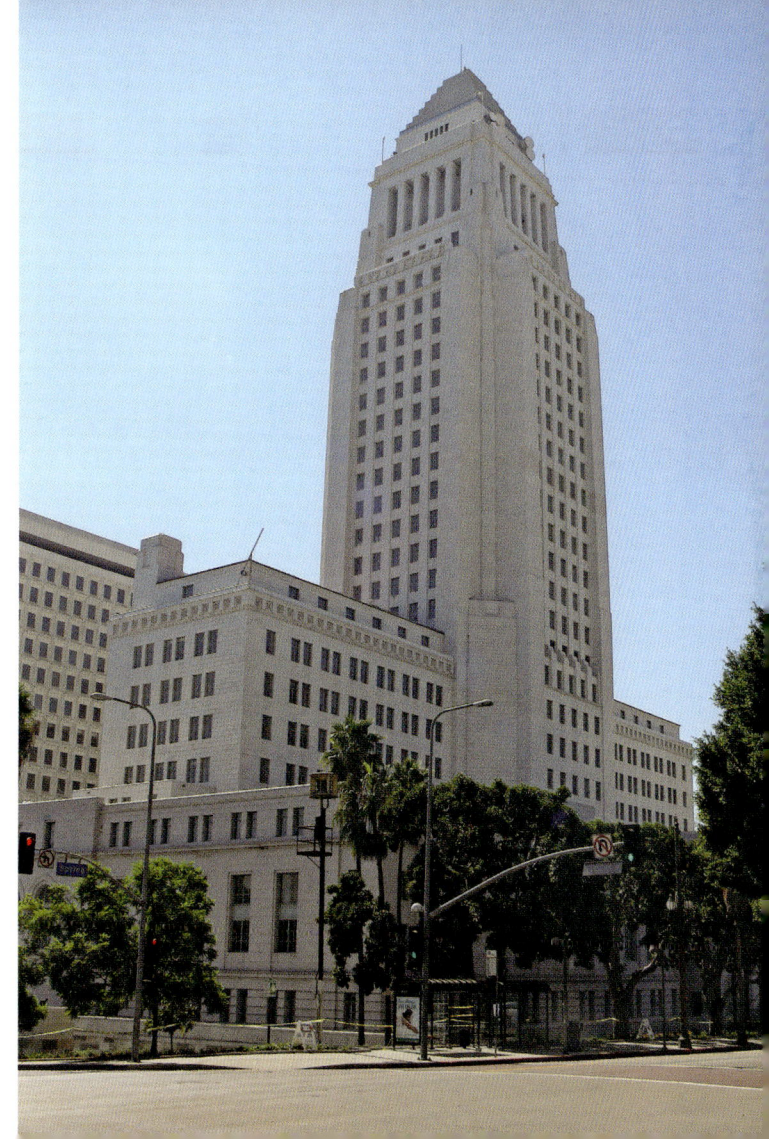

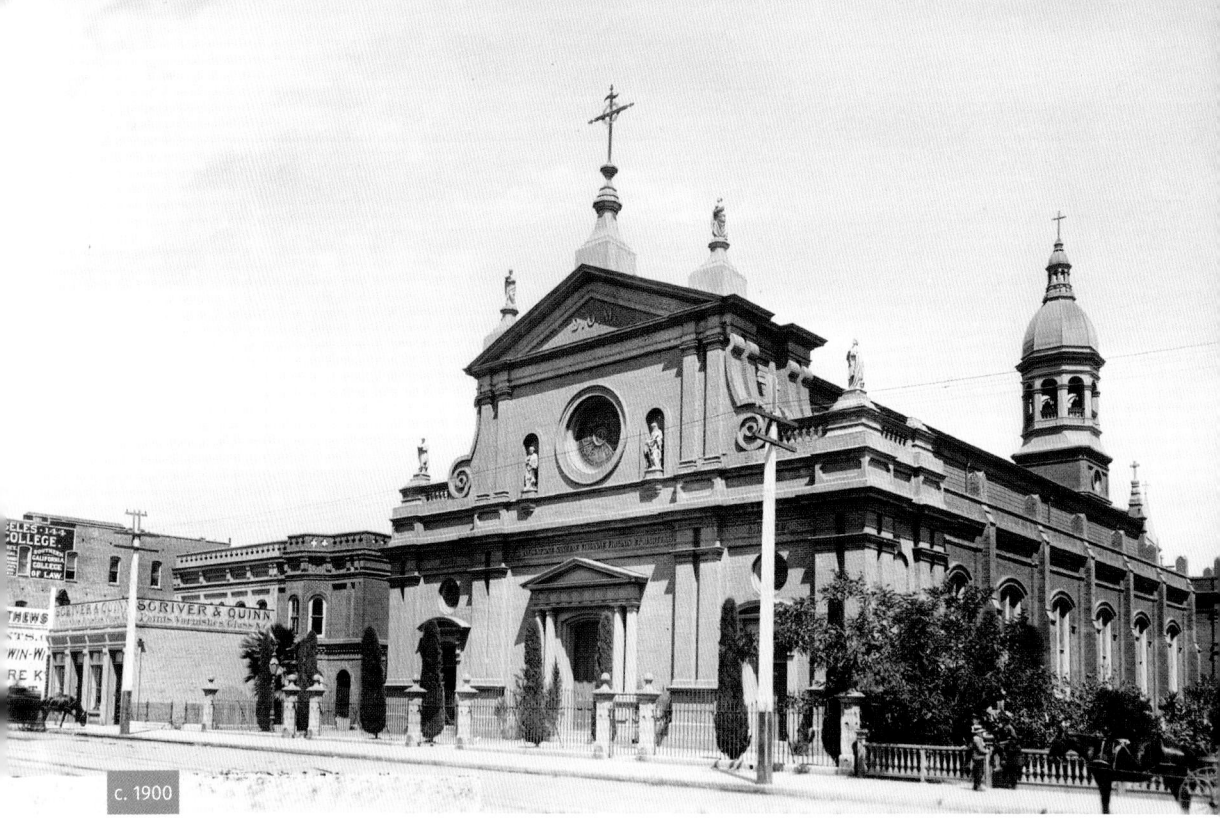

c. 1900

CATHEDRAL OF ST. VIBIANA

The cathedral survived an archdiocese that wanted it torn down

ABOVE: The Cathedral of St. Vibiana, seat of the Los Angeles Archdiocese, was completed in 1876 when Los Angeles's population reached 5,500—3,000 of whom were Catholics. Designed by Ezra Kysor, it was modeled after a Baroque church in Barcelona, on land donated by Amiel Cavalier at a cost of $80,000—and seated well over a thousand. Inside, preserved in a marble sarcophagus, are the relics of the early Christian martyr St. Vibiana.

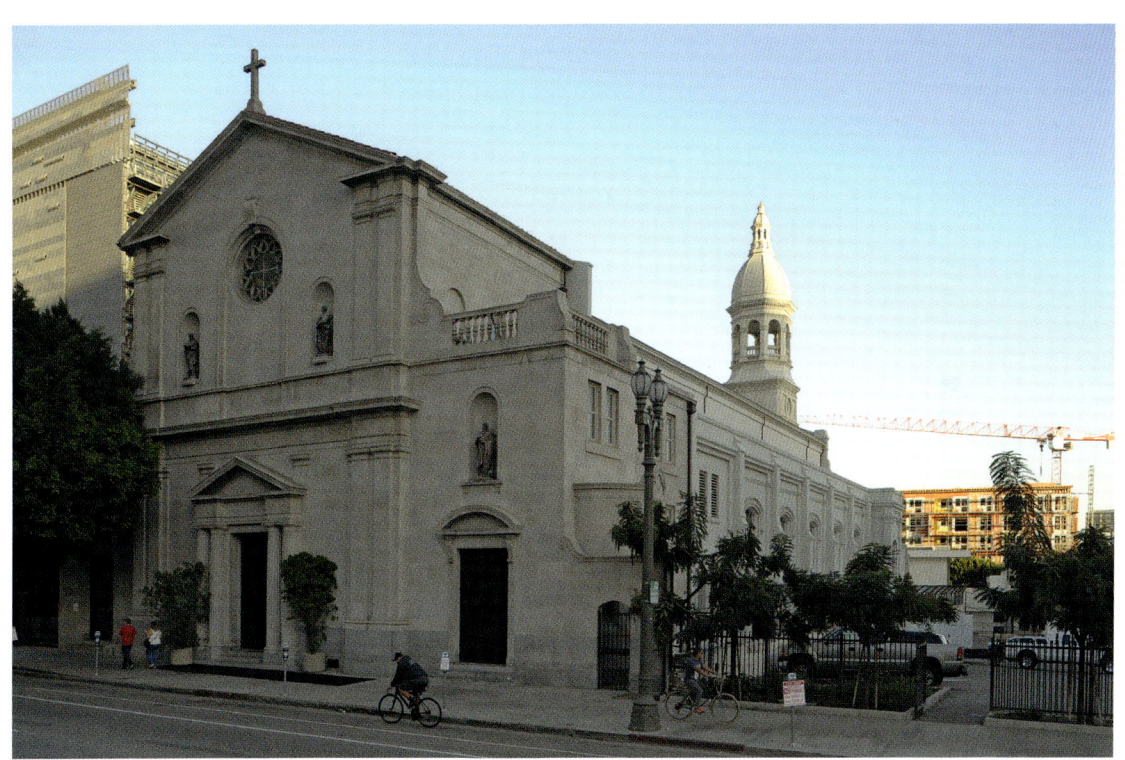

ABOVE: The Cathedral of St. Vibiana was severely damaged by earthquakes in 1971 and 1994. The neglected cathedral was closed in 1995. The archdiocese proposed St. Vibiana's be torn down and a new cathedral built. After much public protest, St. Vibiana's was saved and bought by developer Tom Gilmore for use as a performing arts center. The ultra modern Cathedral of Our Lady of the Angels was built on the corner of Temple and Grand Avenue at a cost said to be in excess of $200 million—$6 million was spent carefully restoring the newly named Vibiana, which is a thriving cultural center, hosting art exhibits, fashion shows, and conferences. The gilded foyer and large main hall—with baroque columns, century-old marble, and a grand stage—now have high-tech sound and lighting systems.

23

FARMERS AND MERCHANTS BANK
The first incorporated bank in Los Angeles, it is the last surviving example of a Beaux-Arts bank

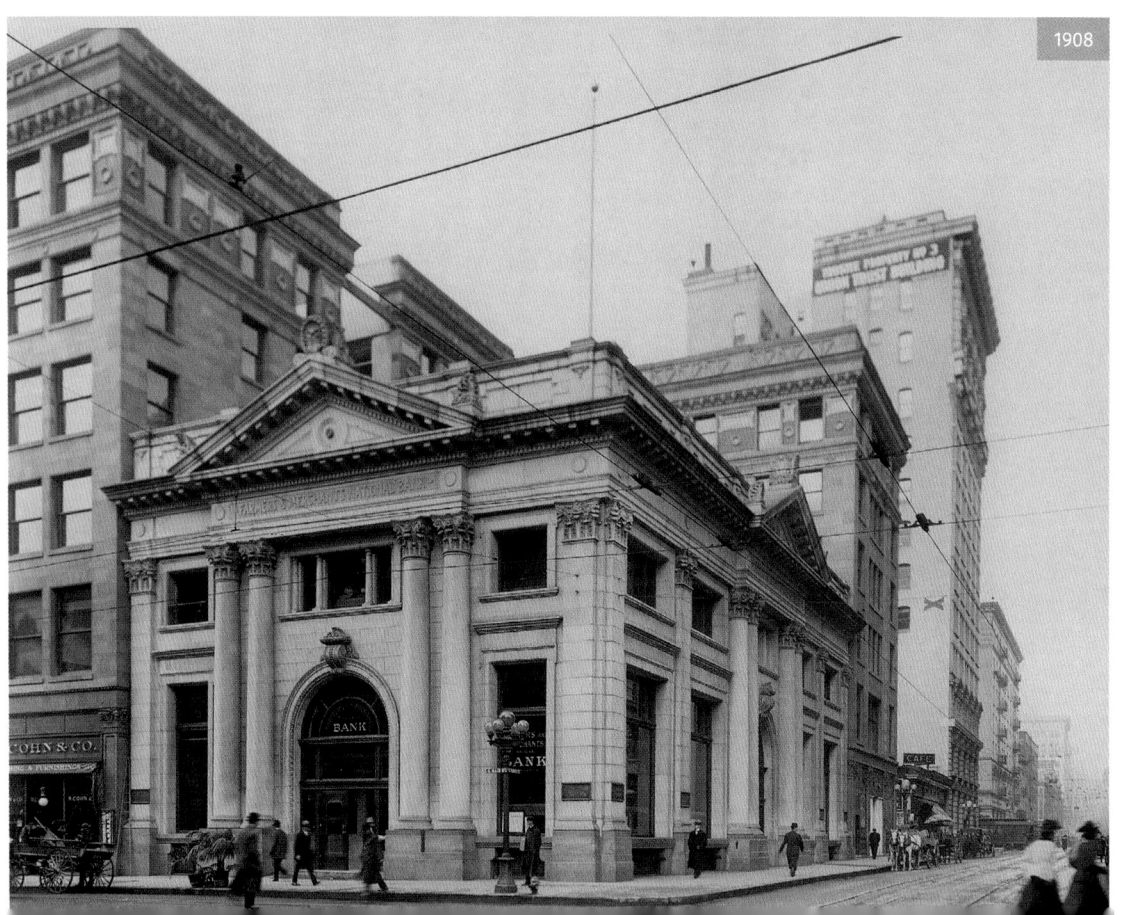

1908

LEFT: The Farmers and Merchants Bank, founded by Isaias Hellman in 1871, was the first incorporated bank in Los Angeles. Photographed in 1908, the Farmers and Merchants Bank on the corner of Main and Fourth Streets was built in 1905 and was designed by the firm of Morgan and Wells. Hellman, a real-estate speculator, merchant, and banker, remained president of the bank until his death in 1920.

BELOW: The last surviving example of a Beaux-Arts banking temple, the Farmers and Merchants Bank operated as a bank until its closure in the late 1980s. This Historic-Cultural Monument was restored to its former elegance. The original banking room, loggia, and central skylight remain, with luxurious loft apartments, art studios, galleries, and banquet facilities. The Romanesque facade and interior are frequently used for filming as well as for social events.

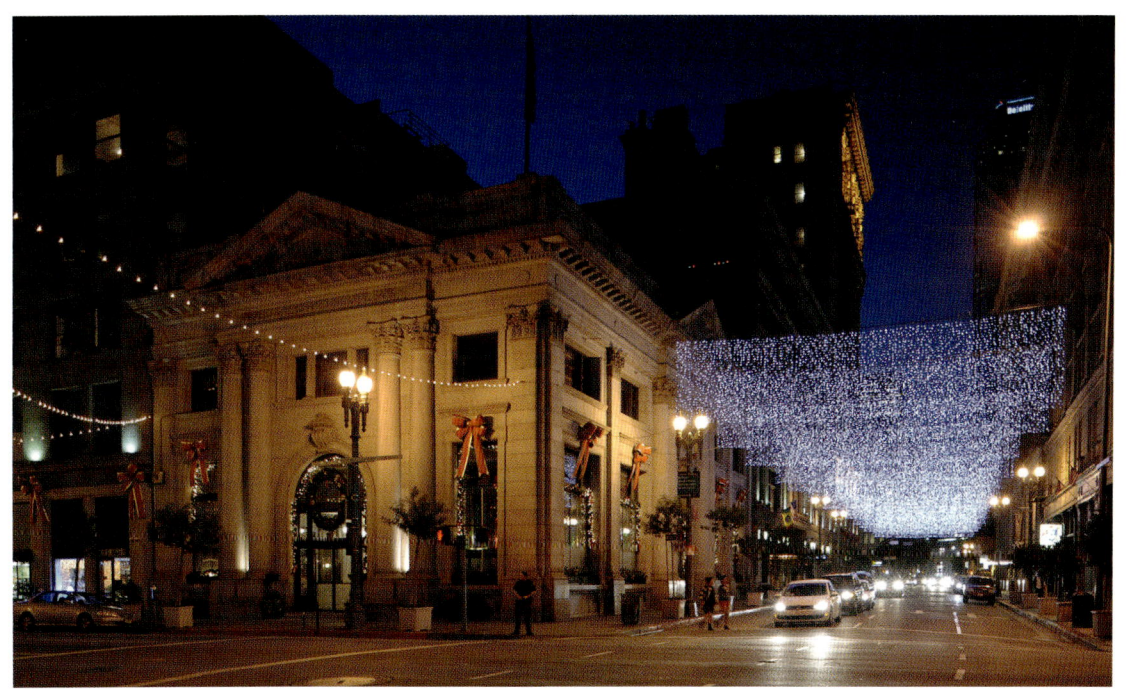

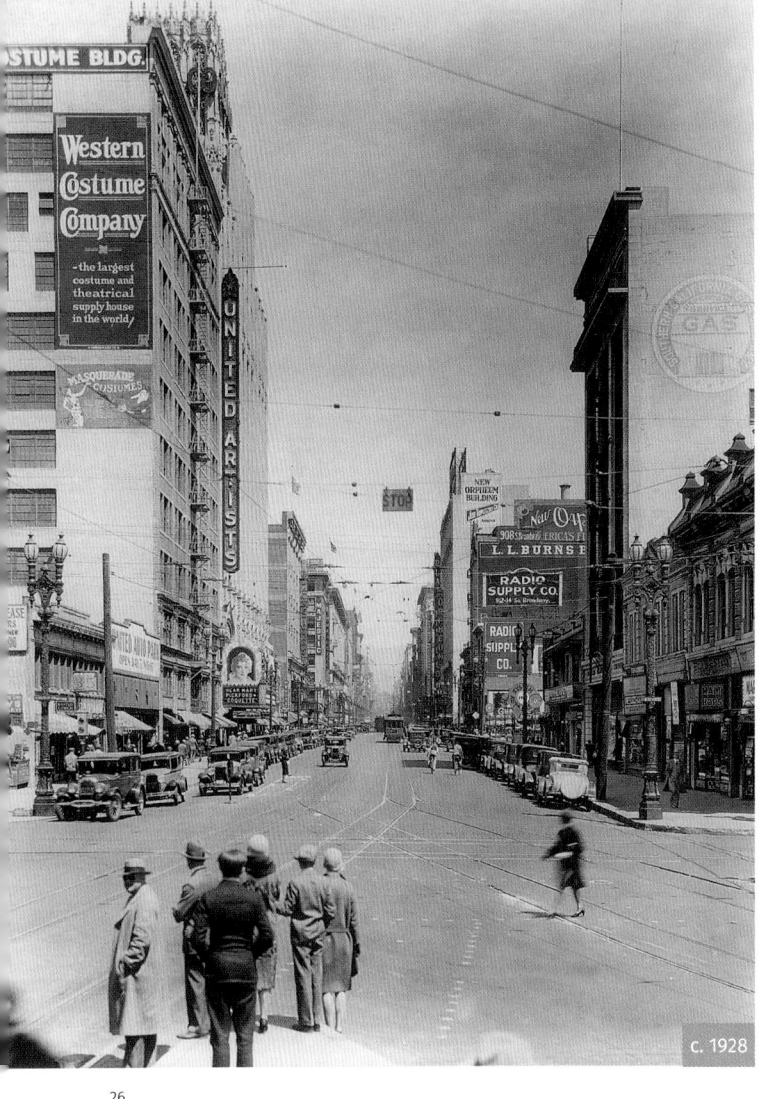

c. 1928

BROADWAY FROM OLYMPIC
Home to the Broadway Theater District

LEFT: Broadway originally started out as a dirt road named Eternity Street, so called because it led to a cemetery. Renamed in 1890, Broadway was the main entertainment street in downtown Los Angeles until the 1960s. Seen here in 1928, it boasted the most vaudeville and movie palaces in the country. The United Artists Theatre opened on December 26, 1927, with *My Best Girl*, starring theater owner Mary Pickford. Pickford and her husband Douglas Fairbanks, who co-owned the United Artists Theatre, showed their lavish films here. The Eastern Columbia Building at 849 South Broadway rivals City Hall as one of the finest surviving examples of Art Deco architecture in the city. Just across the street from the Orpheum Theatre, it was designed by Claud Beelman and opened on September 12, 1930. It served as the new headquarters of the Eastern Outfitting Company and the Columbia Outfitting Company, furniture and clothing stores.

RIGHT: As people and businesses moved west, Broadway was gradually abandoned and neglected. A largely immigrant population of vendors took over the elaborate old theaters of the 1920s. The sumptuous movie palaces became discount shops and flea markets. The Spanish Gothic–style United Artists Theatre became Gene Scott's University Cathedral with a "Jesus Saves" sign overhead—until 2011. New owners renovated the entire building and opened the Ace Hotel in January 2014. They refurbished the United Artists Theatre, which is used for special events and rented out for filming. This was part of the resurgence of downtown Los Angeles and the ten-year "Bringing Back Broadway" plan. With the conversion of many old buildings to loft apartments, the downtown area now had over 45,000 more local inhabitants. Many of the young residents supported the restorations and have introduced new, creative art and performance venues, merging the two worlds. This is bringing people back not just to the theaters but to the streets of downtown Los Angeles, the home to the largest surviving group of pre–World War II theaters. The Eastern Building was listed as a Los Angeles Historic-Cultural Monument in 1985.

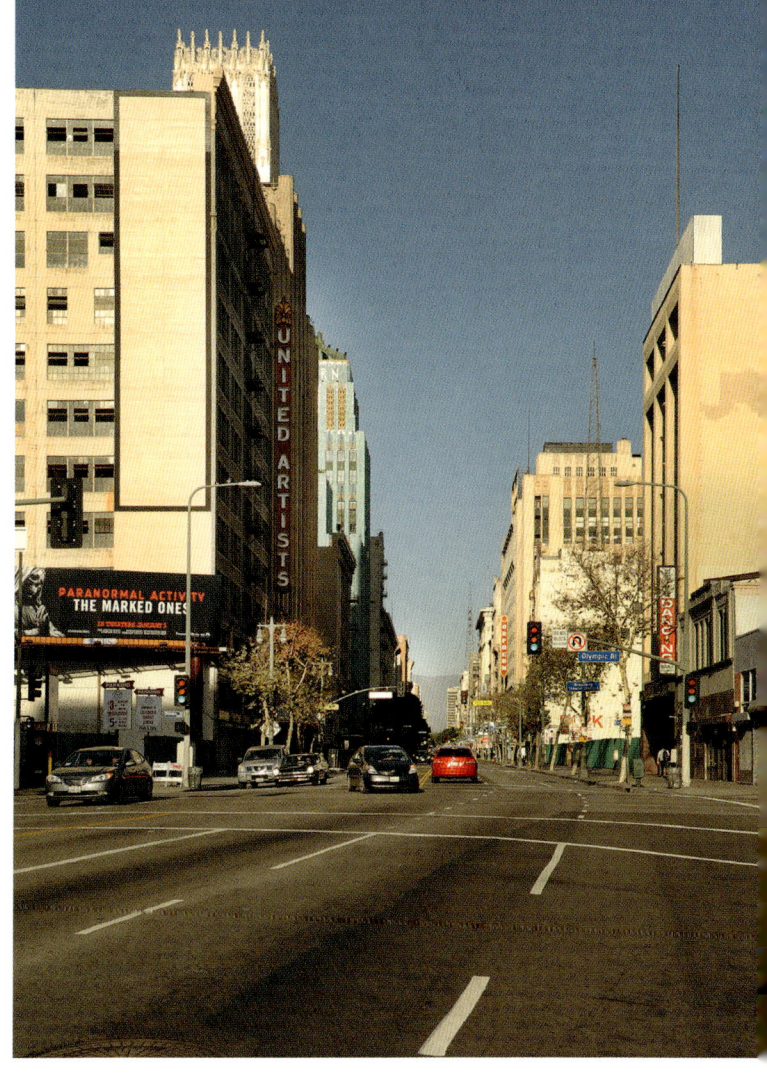

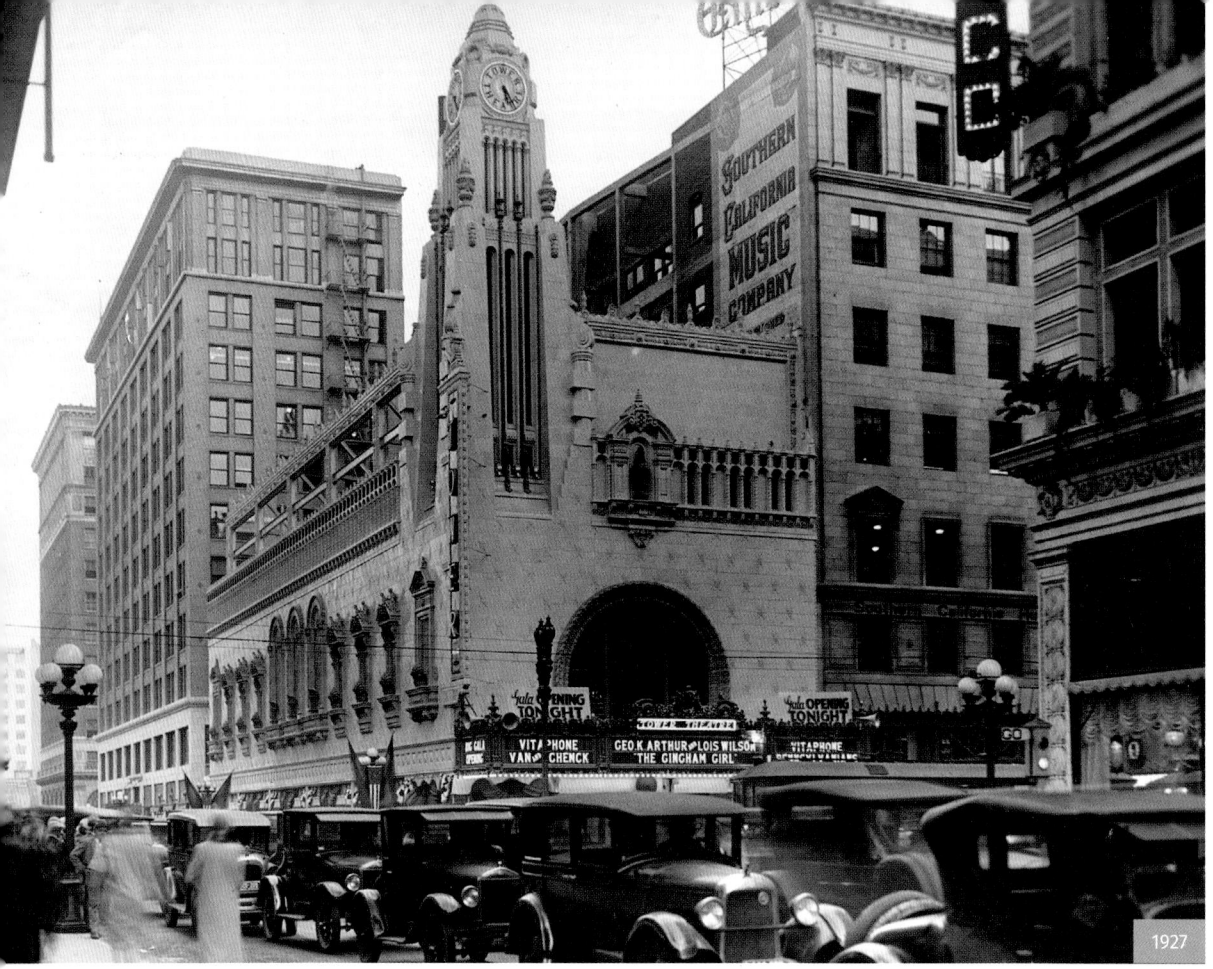

1927

TOWER THEATRE

The first downtown theater to welcome in the talkies

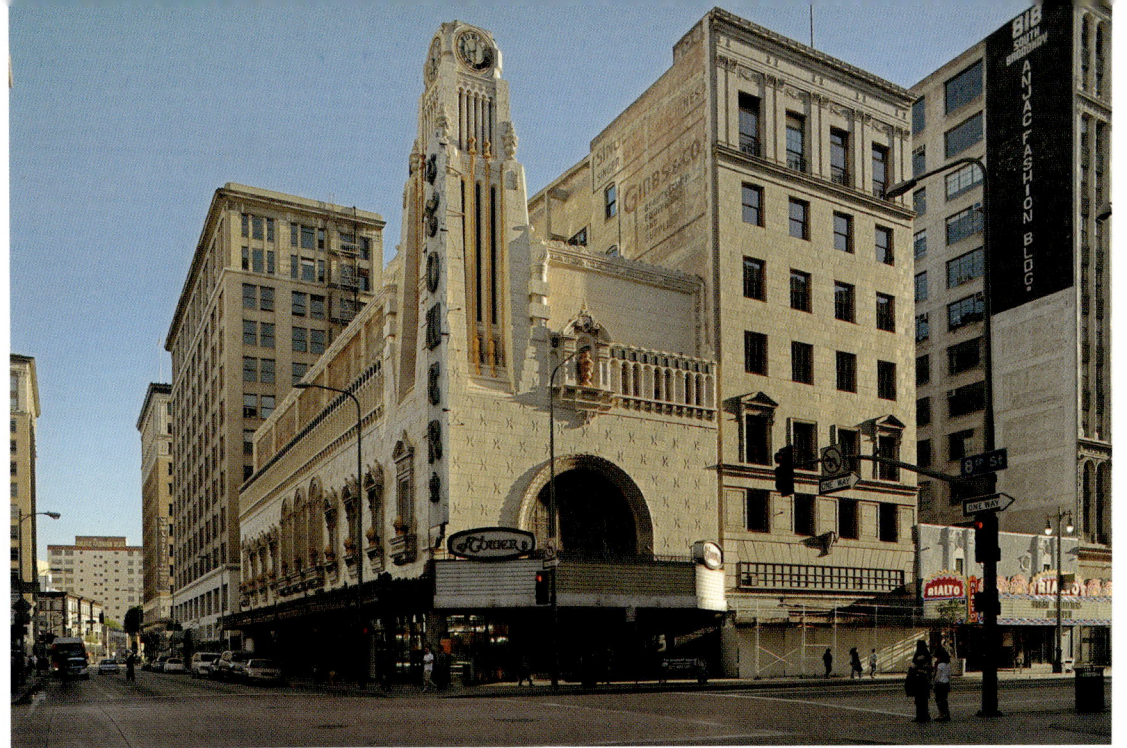

LEFT: Previously the site of the Hyman Theatre (later renamed the Garrick Theatre) built in 1911, the Tower Theatre opened its doors in 1927. It was architect S. Charles Lee's first theater design. Lee was just twenty-eight at the time, but would go on to design around 400 theaters. Seating 1,000 on a tiny site, it was built in a Baroque style with innovative French, Spanish, Moorish, and Italian elements all executed in terra-cotta. The theater was equipped with a Wurlitzer 2 manual ten-rank theater organ. The top of the clock tower was removed after the 1932 Jalisco earthquake. This was the first downtown theater to play "talkies."

ABOVE: Like many other theaters on Broadway, the Tower Theatre was abandoned for many years. It remained mostly intact, but rundown, with its famous tower still standing. The lobby was rented to vendors and the theater was used for filming *Mulholland Drive*, *Fight Club*, and *The Prestige*, among others. The Living Faith Evangelical Church rented the venue until the Delijani family bought the Tower, the Palace, the Los Angeles and the State Theatres, forming The Broadway Theatre Group. The multi-million dollar revitalization planned for the Tower Theatre is still "a work in progress."

MAYAN THEATRE

Opened as a conventional theater, the Mayan soon started showing movies

BELOW: The Belasco and Mayan Theatres were designed by the architectural firm of Morgan, Walls, and Clements and opened as conventional theaters in 1926 and 1927, respectively. The owners were hoping to establish a new theater district west of Broadway with the Mayan at 1040 South Hill and the Belasco at 1050 South Hill. The Belasco's opening production was the comedy *Gentlemen Prefer Blondes* (with an advertisement visible on the side of the building until it was repainted in 2006) while the Mayan opened with the musical comedy *Oh Kay.* starring Elsie Janis. By 1929 the Mayan had started showing movies and in 1931 it was being billed as Grauman's Mayan.

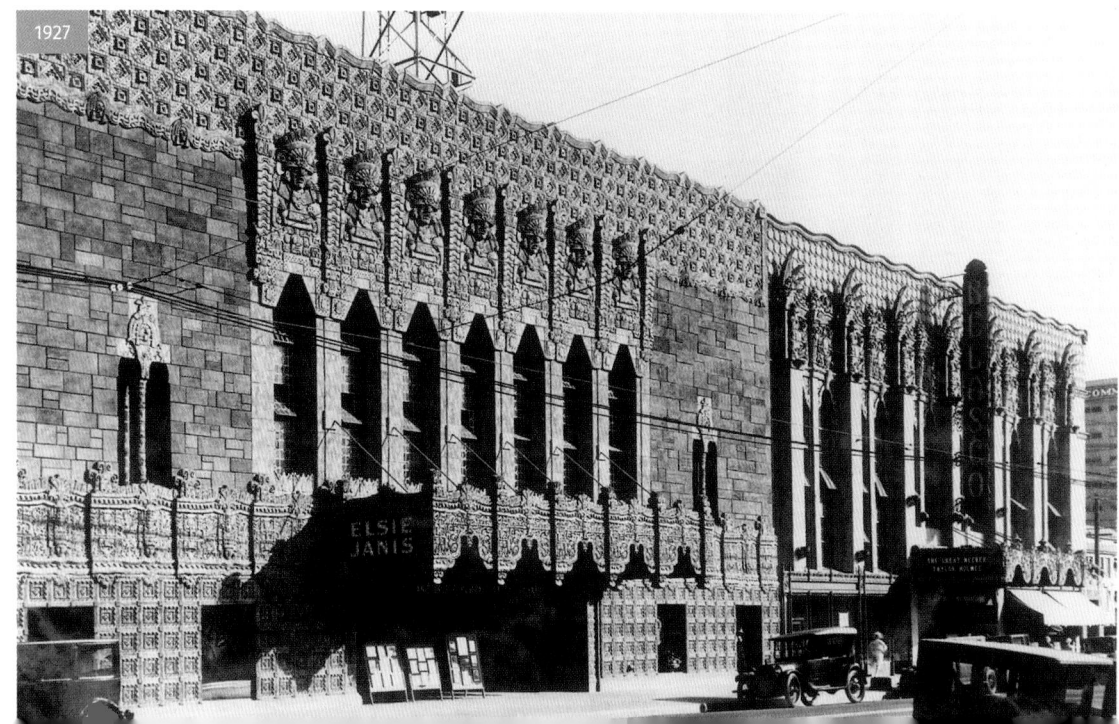

1927

BELOW: Legitimate theater wasn't abandoned at the Mayan, and as part of the WPA Federal Theater Project in the 1930s it put on shows such as *Follow the Parade* and *Volpone*. It switched between stage shows and Spanish-language films in the 1940s and 1950s. Duke Ellington played 101 shows to an unsegregated audience here starting in 1941, a time when audiences were segregated downtown. The 1960s and 1970s proved to be hard times, and in the early 1970s it started to show adult movies (some of which were shot in the basement). In 1977 the auditorium was split into three screens—still showing adult movies—until 1990, when the venue became the Mayan nightclub, which it remains today. The neighboring Belasco was closed in 1952 and subsequently used as a community church. There were plans to convert it into a nightclub, but after a $10 million renovation it reopened as a theater in 2011.

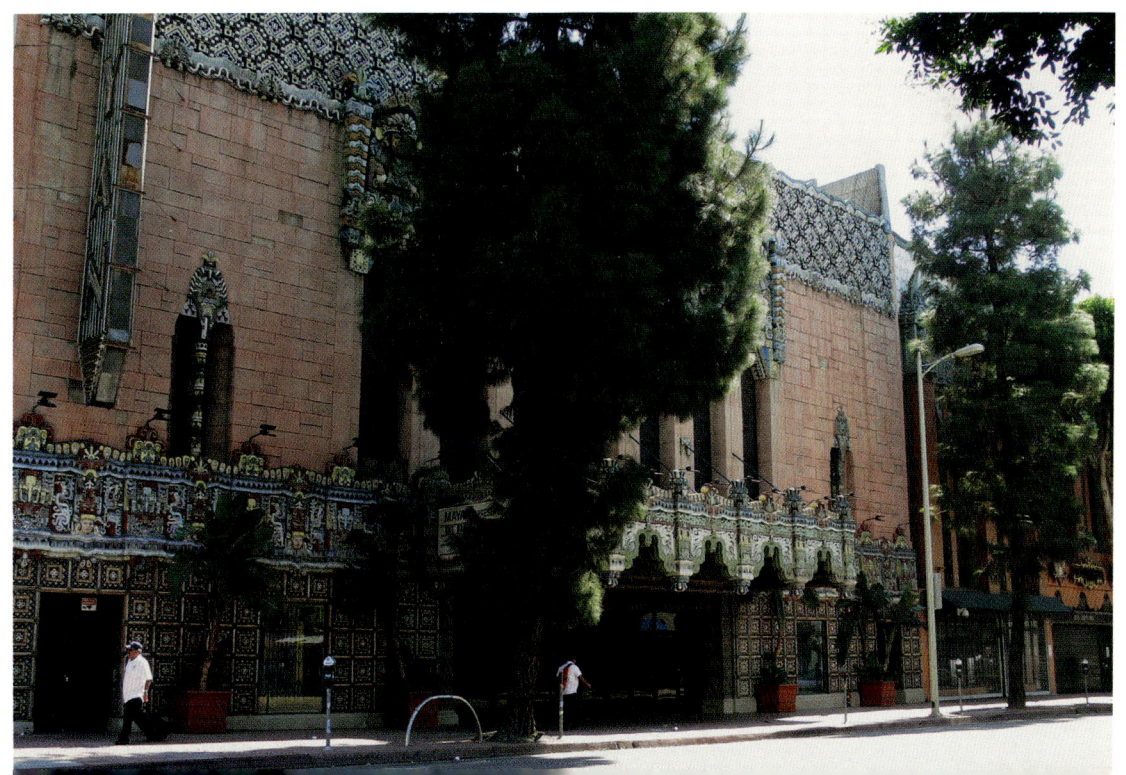

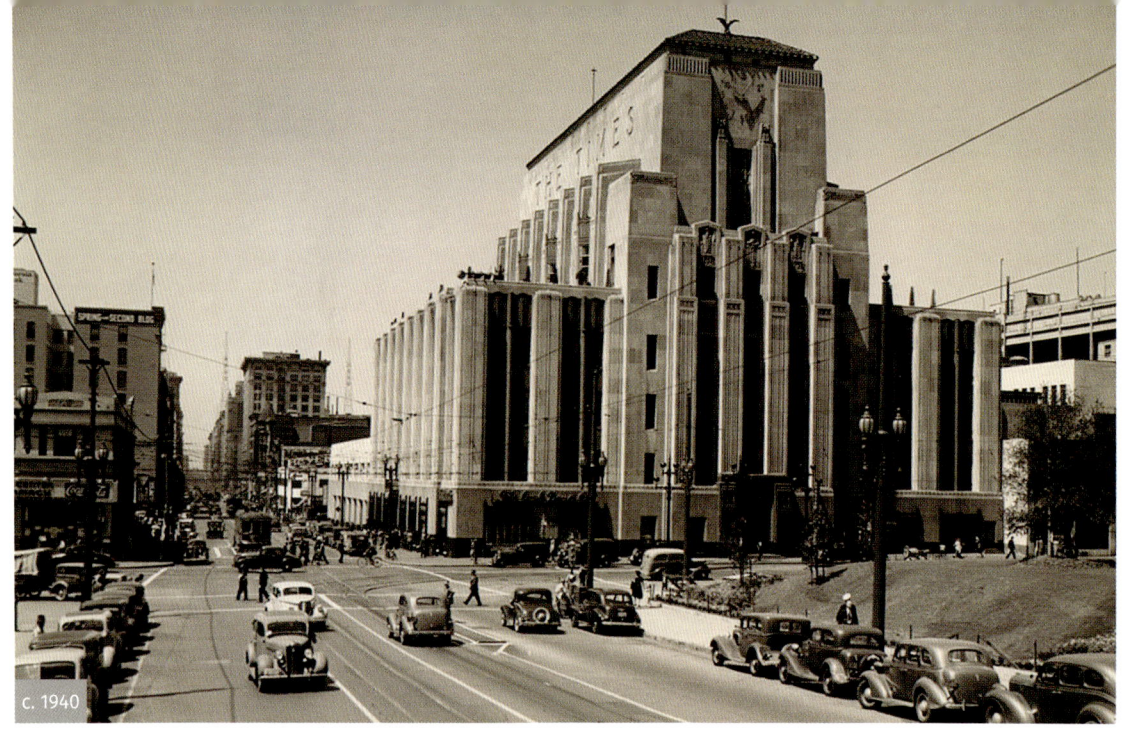

c. 1940

LOS ANGELES TIMES BUILDING

A gold medal winner at the 1937 Paris Exposition

ABOVE: The *Los Angeles Times* newspaper was first published December 4, 1881, in a small brick building at Temple and New High Street. On October 1, 1910, the building was dynamited by union activists, destroying the building, killing twenty-one people, and injuring many. Owner Harrison Gray Otis had been fighting to keep the paper an "open shop" for workers. The paper was then run from a branch office at 531 South Spring Street. Otis died in 1917 and Harry Chandler, his son-in-law, became the second publisher of the *Times*. The new Art Deco Los Angeles Times Building opened in 1935 on the corner of First and Spring Streets. At the time, it was the largest building on the West Coast used entirely for newspaper publishing. Designed by Gordon B. Kaufman, it won a gold medal at the 1937 Paris Exposition for its modern architectural style. The Globe Lobby had ten-foot-high murals painted by Hugo Ballin in 1934.

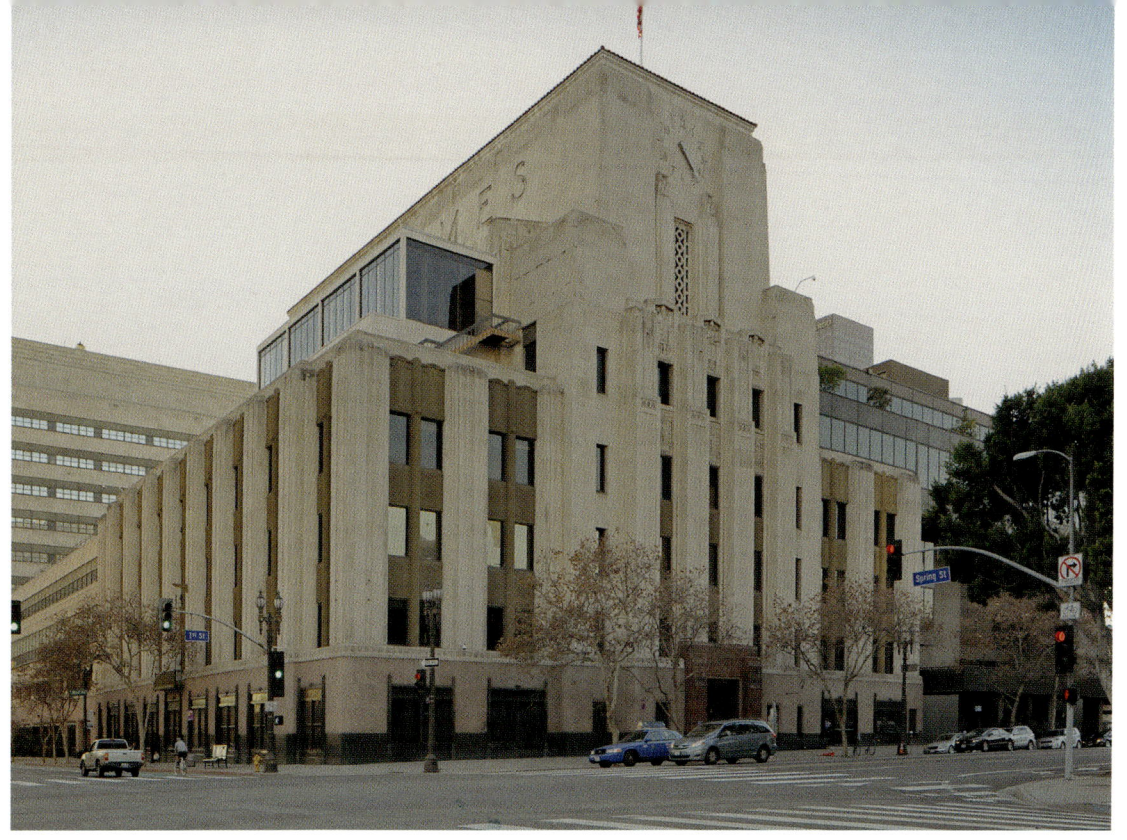

ABOVE: In 1989, following the closure of rival paper the *Herald-Examiner*, the *Times* hired many *Herald* staffers, bought their subscription list, and took over several *Herald* features. The following year, the *Times'* circulation reached an all-time high. In June 2002, the *Times* merged with the *Chicago Tribune* and became part of a large media group. The lobby featured an historical exhibit showcasing the first 100 years of the Times. In June 2017, the Art Deco building was sold for $120 million to a Canadian company, the Omni Group. They have received permission to demolish ancillary buildings to create two new towers, whilst leaving the 1937 building intact. Despite its heritage, the Times Building is not a Los Angeles Historic-Cultural Monument. The newspaper staff moved out in 2018 to an office building in El Segundo.

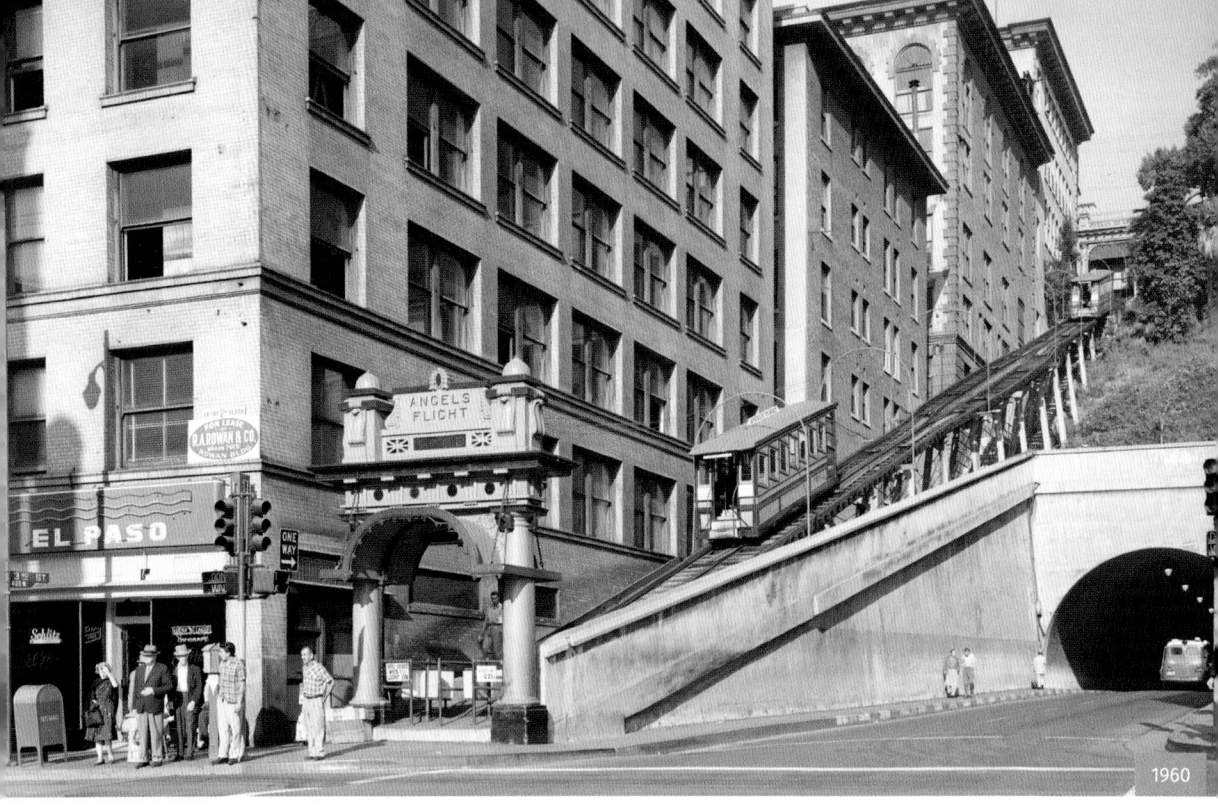

1960

ANGEL'S FLIGHT

The world's shortest railroad is back in business

ABOVE: In 1901 J. W. Eddy built the Los Angeles Incline Railway at Third and Hill Streets to connect downtown with the upper-class residential area of Bunker Hill. Soon renamed Angel's Flight and dubbed "the world's shortest railroad," its two counterbalancing white cars, Sinai and Olivet (named after biblical mountains), descended and ascended the hill for one penny each way until 1953, when the price was raised to a nickel for a round-trip. The archway was added in 1908, and in 1930 the cars were painted orange and black.

34

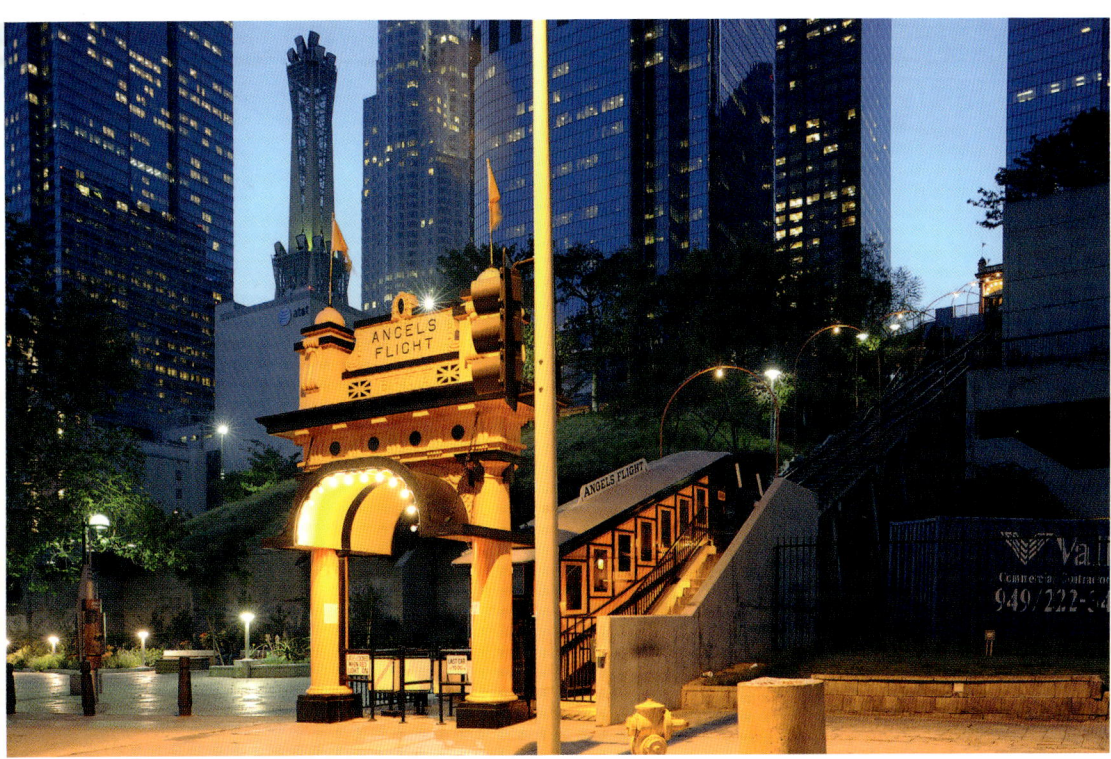

ABOVE: By the 1960s, Bunker Hill had become rundown and was replaced with office buildings and a senior citizens' housing complex. Angel's Flight was dismantled and stored. Thirty years later, in 1996, the new Angel's Flight was installed just half a block south of the original location. At twenty-five cents a ride, the funicular was highly popular until a fatal accident occurred in February 2001 and it was closed for repair. Angel's Flight reopened in 2010. Taken out of service yet again, the iconic funicular reopened on Labor Day, September 4, 2017, after a closure to install further safety systems. Rides are now a dollar. During the closure, Ryan Gosling and Emma Stone were seen in the historic carriage for the film *La La Land*. The Angel's Flight Railway Foundation operates the 116-year-old railway.

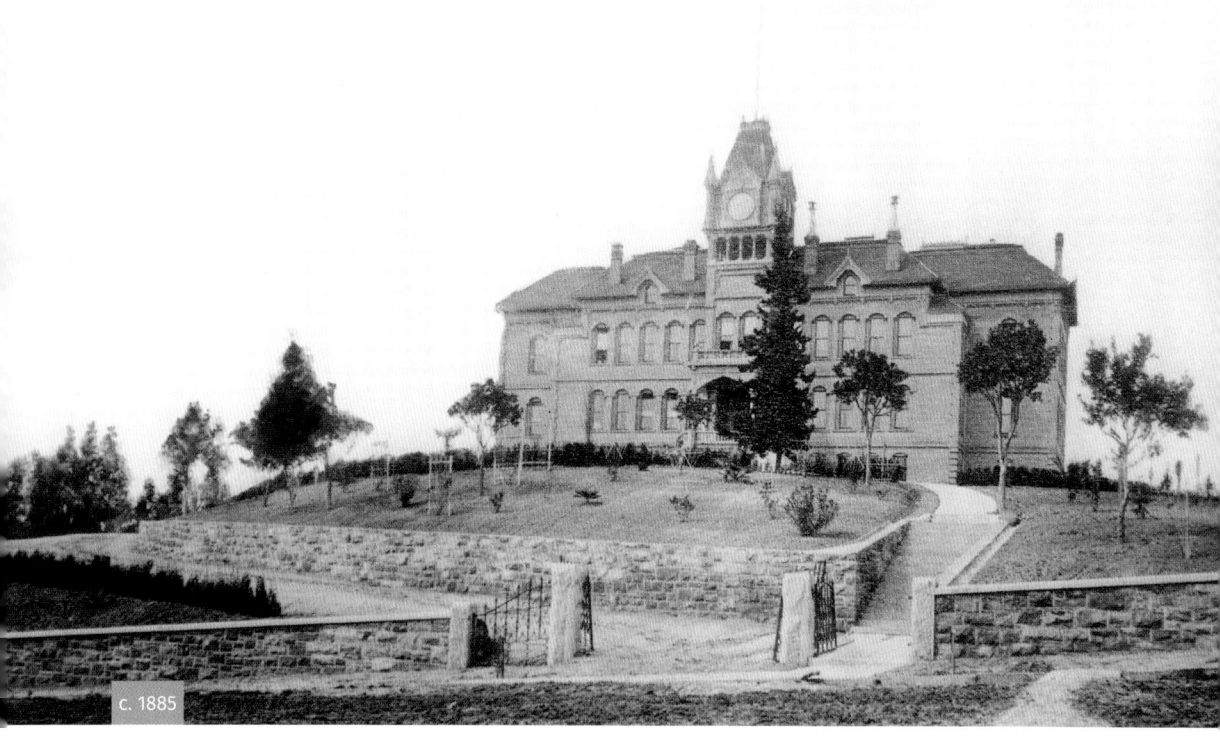

c. 1885

STATE NORMAL SCHOOL / L.A. PUBLIC LIBRARY

A unique building, the 1926 library displays many architectural styles

ABOVE: In the 1880s, the growing population of Los Angeles needed a place of learning, and in 1882 the State Normal School opened and welcomed its first students, most of whom were women. By 1914 the school had moved to a larger facility on Vermont Avenue. It continued to grow, and in 1919 the newly named Southern Branch of the University of Los Angeles (later UCLA) began a search for a larger site, which was eventually found in Westwood. The original school site at Fifth and Grand became the home of the Los Angeles Public Library.

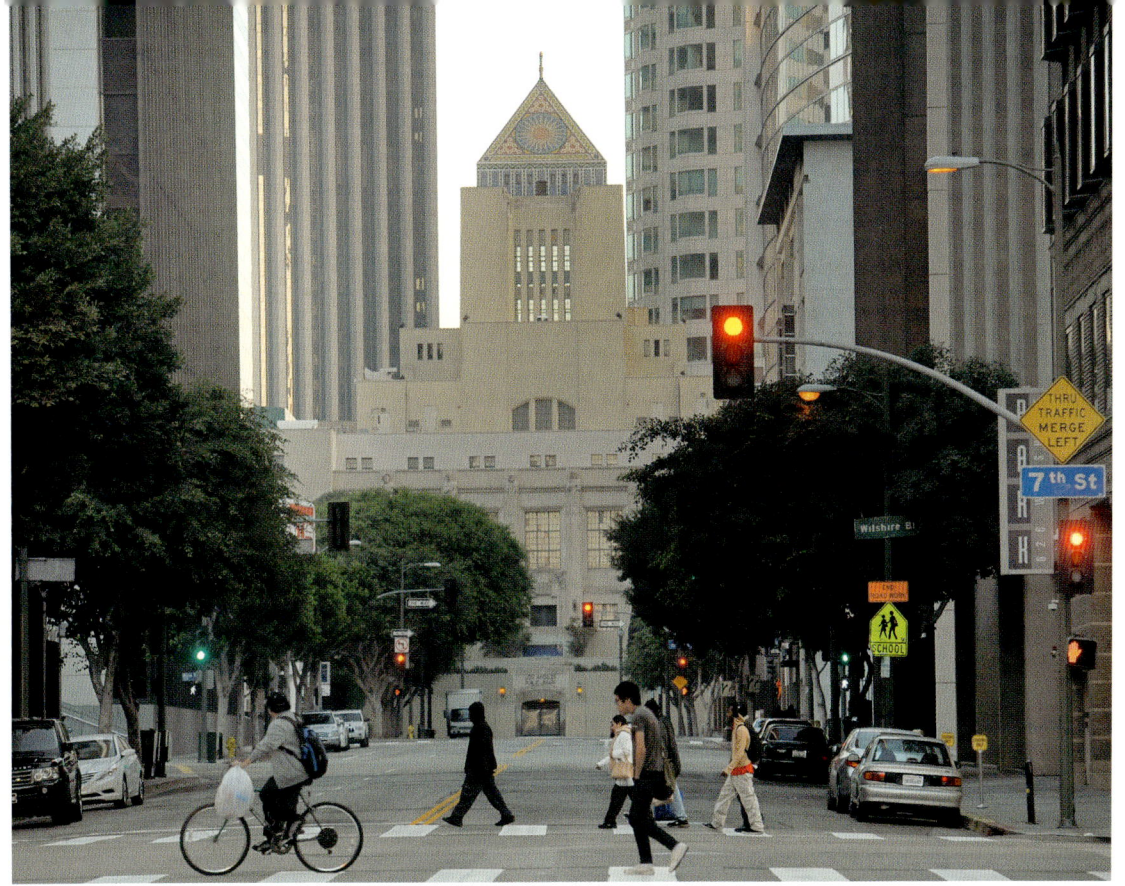

ABOVE: The new Central Library Building, specially designed by Bertram Goodhue, opened in 1926 with numerous entrances, tide pools, and lawns. These were gradually reduced with the growth of downtown and the need for parking space. After two arson fires in the 1980s, the library was restored at a cost of $125 million and expanded with four stories above and four stories and parking underground, as well as a stunning rear atrium. The archives include over three million historic photographs and a 2012 donation of over a million maps. The library facade looks just as it did in 1926.

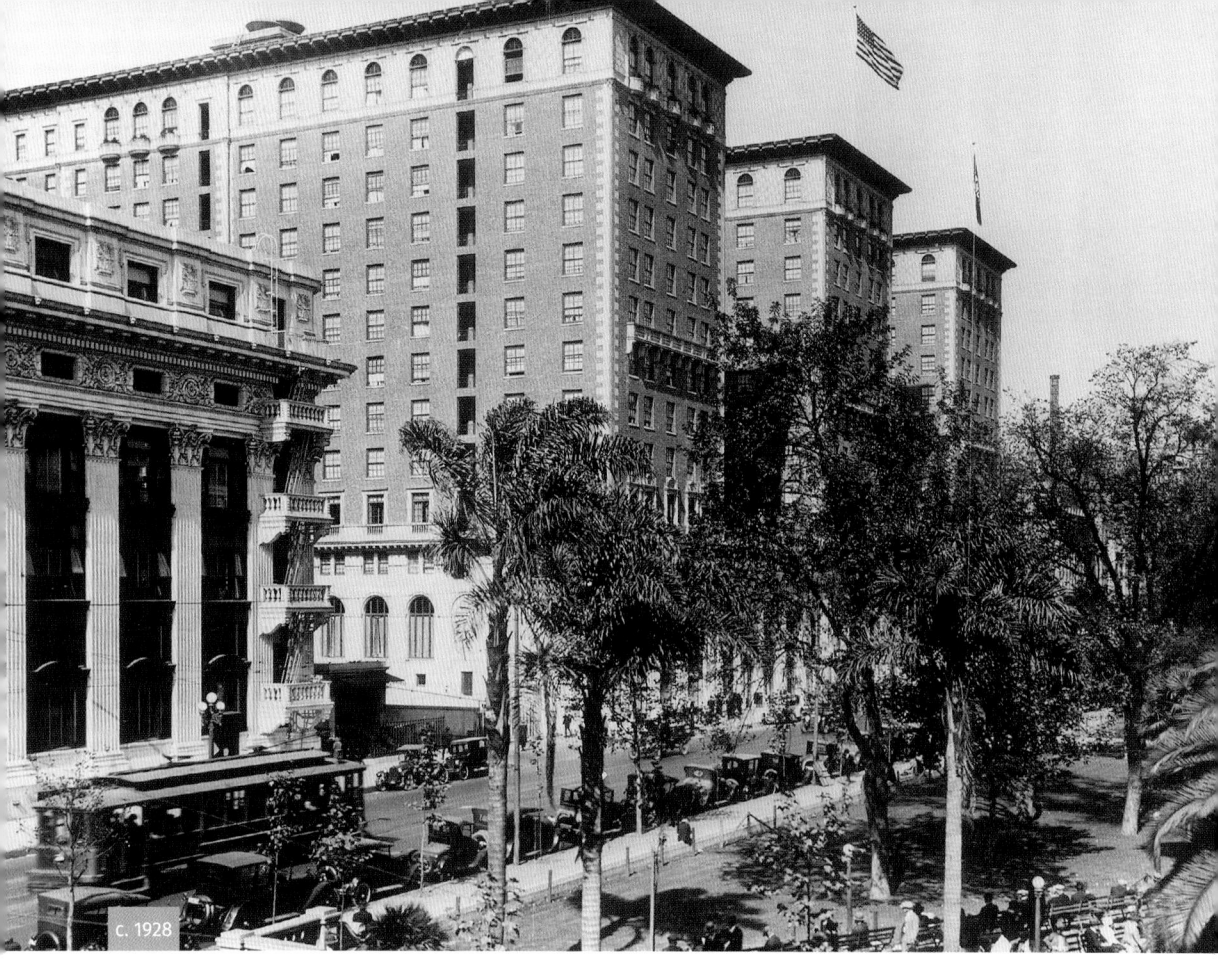
c. 1928

BILTMORE HOTEL
An early home for the Academy Awards ceremony

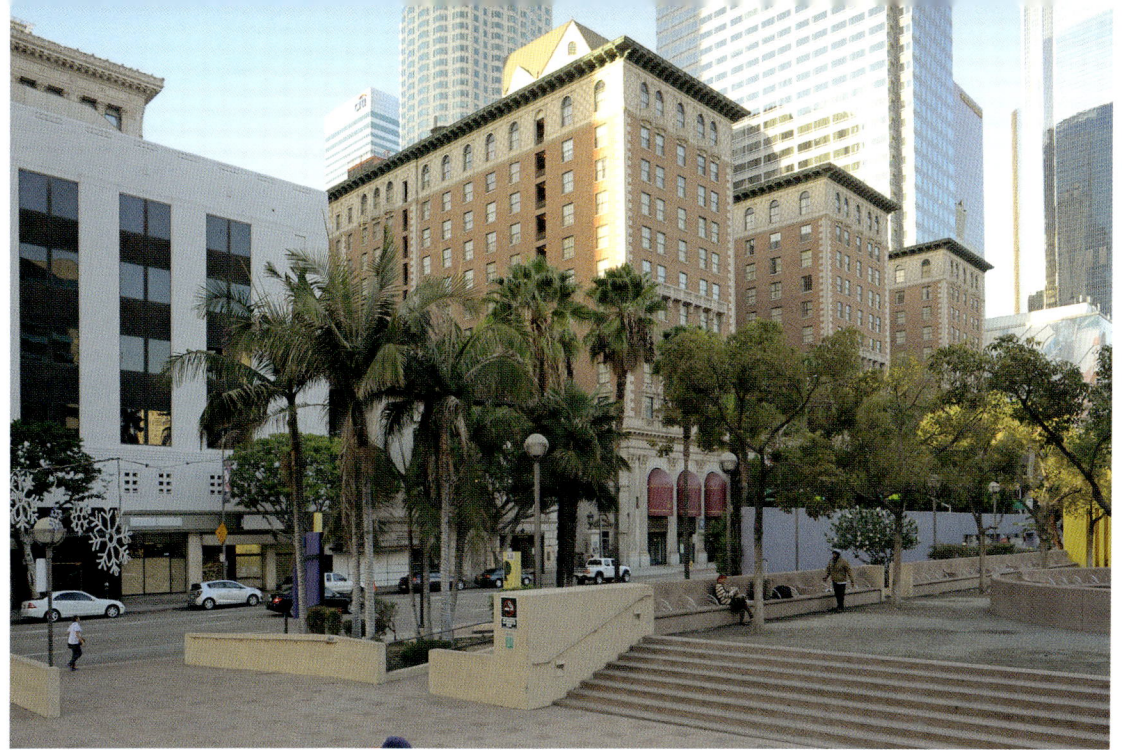

LEFT: At 506 South Grand Avenue, the Biltmore Hotel towers over Pershing Square. Designed by Schultze and Weaver, the $10-million Biltmore opened on October 1, 1923, with 1,500 rooms. It was the largest hotel west of Chicago at the time. Italian artist Giovanni Smeraldi, known for his work in the Vatican and the White House, was employed to produce frescoes on the ceilings of the main Galleria and the Crystal Ballroom, and a grand Spanish Baroque Revival bronze doorway was installed, complete with an astrological clock. The Academy of Motion Picture Arts and Sciences was founded at a lunch in the Crystal Ballroom.

ABOVE: Foreign royalty and numerous U.S. presidents have slept here. Everything from Academy Award dinners to John F. Kennedy's Democratic Convention have been held here, and the Beatles were once helicoptered onto the hotel roof and hid here for days. With the resurgence of Pershing Square, the hotel—now the Millennium Biltmore—has also had a multimillion-dollar facelift. In October 2013, they held a star-studded ninetieth anniversary celebration. The hotel continues to be a popular location for films and TV shows. Meanwhile, the adjacent Pershing Square has been upgraded with a concert stage.

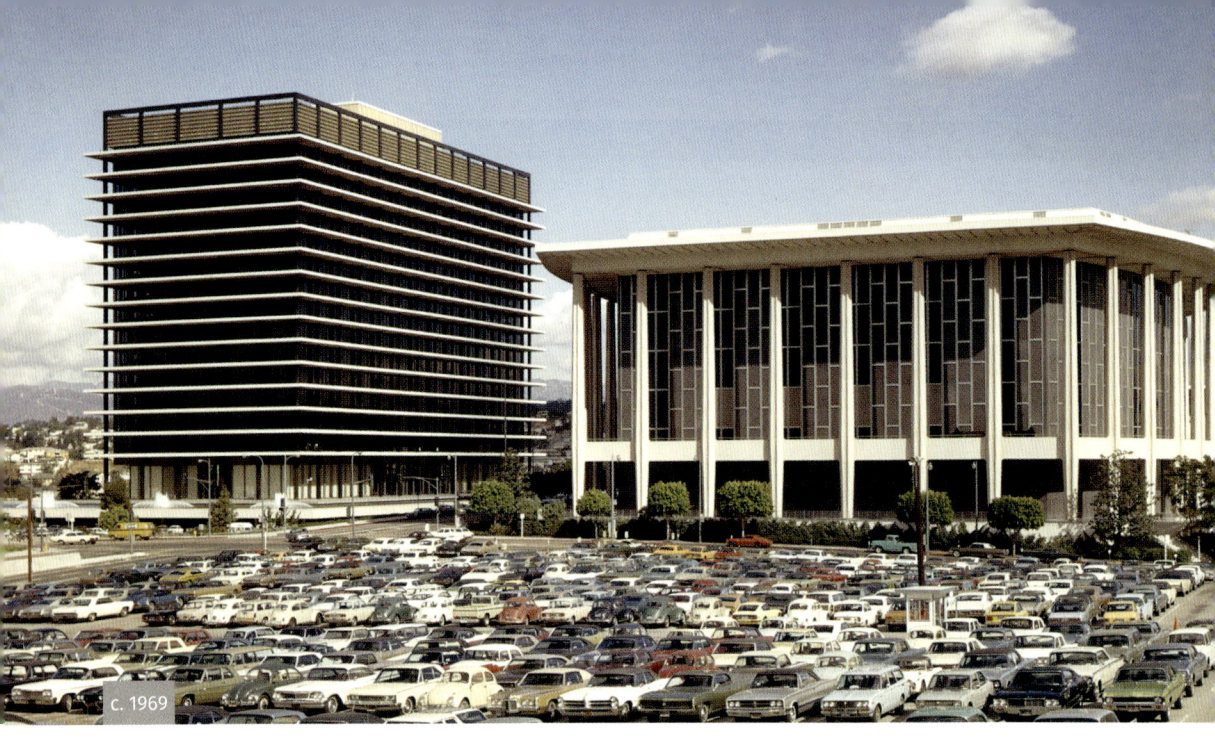

c. 1969

DOROTHY CHANDLER CENTER

The city's Music Center has long been the home of outstanding architecture

ABOVE: The 1964 Dorothy Chandler Pavilion was the first theater to be completed in the Los Angeles Music Center. It was named for Dorothy Buffum Chandler (wife of *Los Angeles Times* owner Norman Chandler), who was seeking a home for the Los Angeles Philharmonic. Designed by Welton Becket, it was the largest theater in the complex with 3,197 seats. A curved building with tall colonnades, the Pavilion has been home to the Christmas Eve Holiday Celebration since 1964. The Los Angeles Master Chorale resided here and the New York City Opera performed regularly. The smaller Ahmanson Theatre opened in 1967 with a production of *Man of La Mancha*. The smaller, 739-seat Mark Taper Forum—also constructed in 1967—has welcomed more experimental productions like *Zoot Suit*, *Children of a Lesser God*, *Shadow Box*, and *Angels in America*.

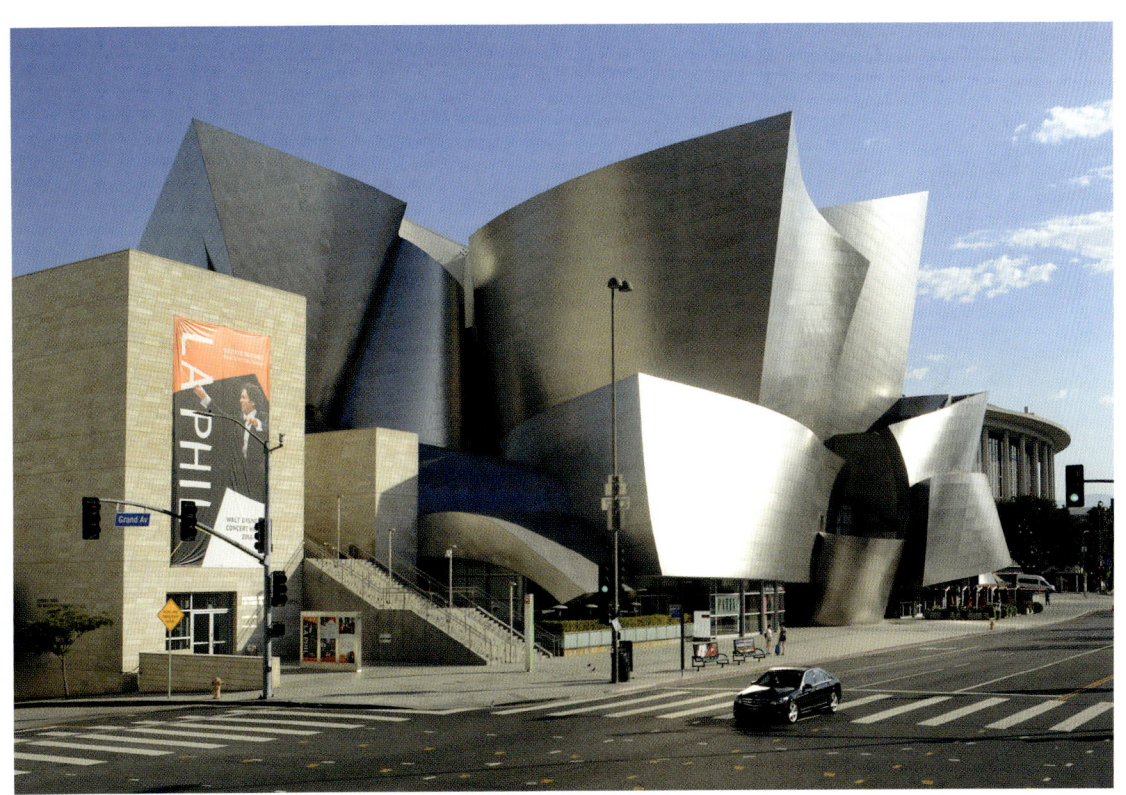

ABOVE: The Los Angeles Music Center added the inspirational, Frank Gehry-designed Walt Disney Concert Hall in October 2003. It sits just outside the original 1960s complex and features 2,265 seats, including the 266-seat Roy Disney Cal Arts Theatre and the outdoor Keck Foundation's Children's Theatre. It is now home to the Los Angeles Philharmonic and Master Chorale. A $41 million renovation of the county-owned Music Center Plaza was completed in 2019. The plaza connects the theaters and restaurants and the redevelopment has enlarged the occupancy of the space from 2,500 to 5,000 people, effectively making it a fifth concert venue.

LOS ANGELES COLISEUM
The stadium with a unique Olympic pedigree

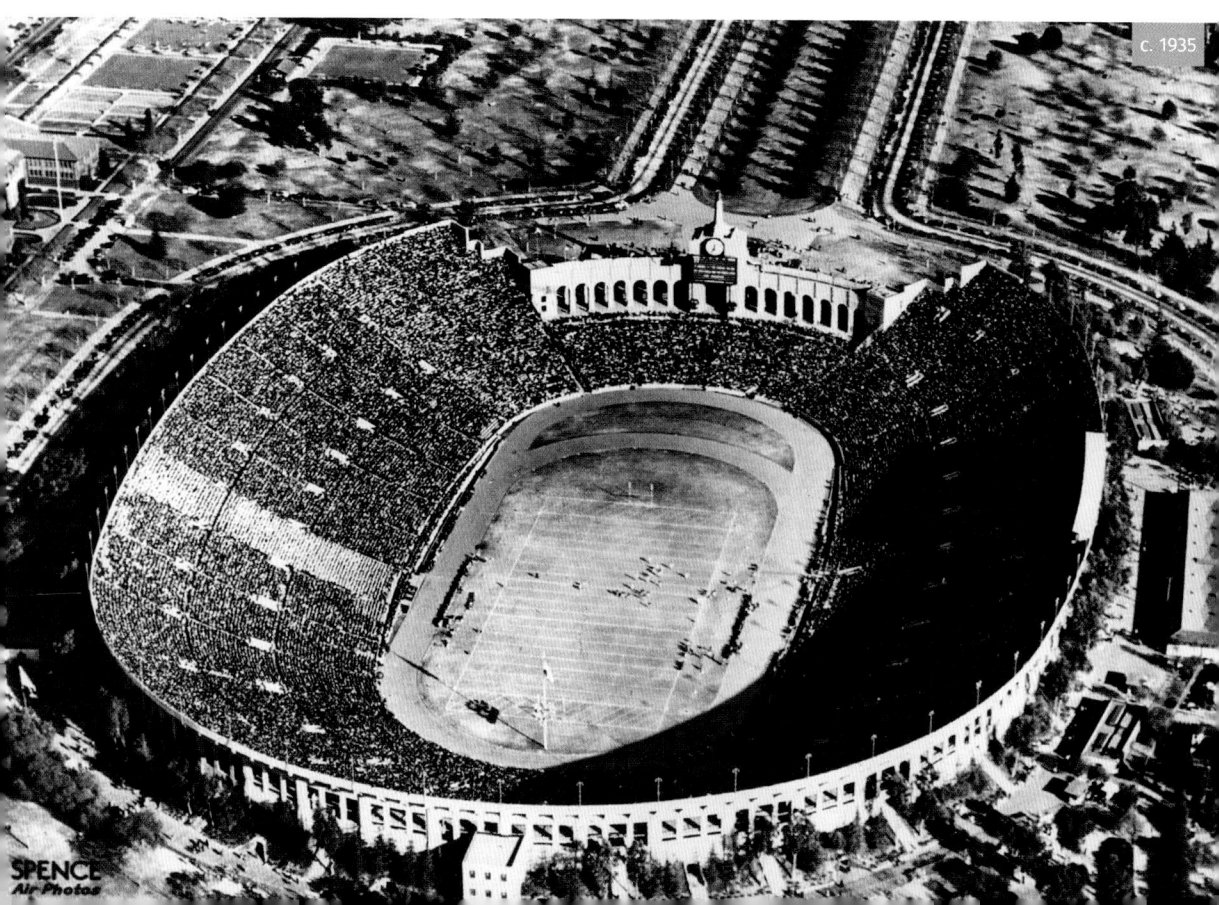

LEFT: Commissioned in 1921 to honor veterans of World War I, the Los Angeles Memorial Coliseum opened in 1923. At a cost of just under $1 million, the venue offered a seating capacity of 75,144. The first football game held in the stadium took place on October 6, 1923, when the University of Southern California beat Pomona College, 23–7. By 1930 Los Angeles had emerged onto the world stage and earned the honor of hosting the 1932 Olympic Games. The city scrambled to accommodate everyone, expanding the Coliseum's seating to 101,574. Fifty-two years later, the stadium did it again, hosting the 1984 Olympics. The Olympic cauldron torch remains on site, as do other Olympic symbols and statues. At the Coliseum's Court of Honor, visitors can learn about Olympic history through plaques and a full list of the 1932 and 1984 gold medalists.

RIGHT: The State of California, Los Angeles County, and the City of Los Angeles jointly own the Los Angeles Memorial Coliseum, located in today's University Park neighborhood. It is the only stadium in the world to have hosted two Olympic Games, as well as the only Olympic stadium to have also hosted the Super Bowl and the World Series. The Coliseum became a National Historic Landmark on July 27, 1984, the day before the opening ceremony of the 1984 Olympics. In dramatic Hollywood fashion, the Olympic cauldron still sees regular use. In solidarity, the torch is lit during Olympics held in other cities. When tragedy strikes, the torch may stay lit for days, as it did after the 1986 space shuttle *Challenger* disaster. The torch burned for a full week after the September 11, 2001 attacks.

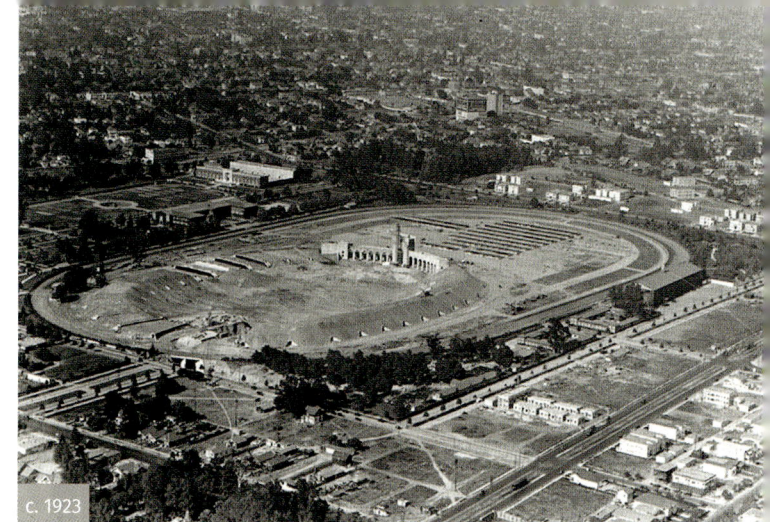

c. 1923

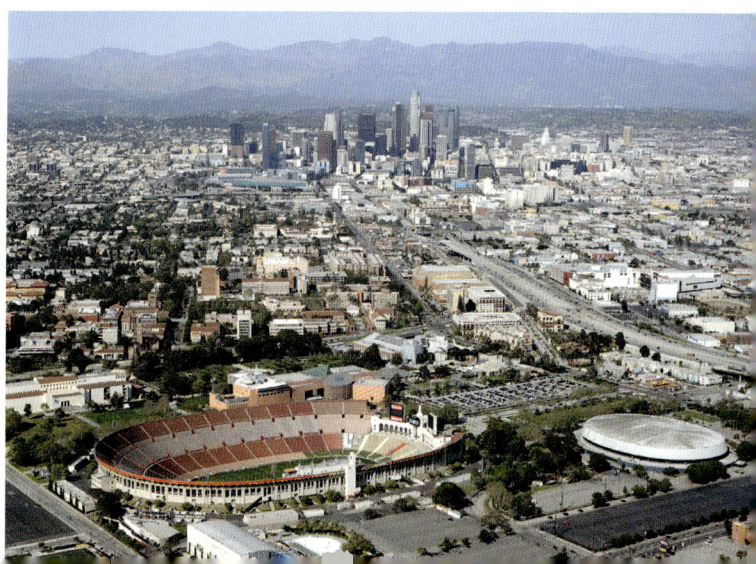

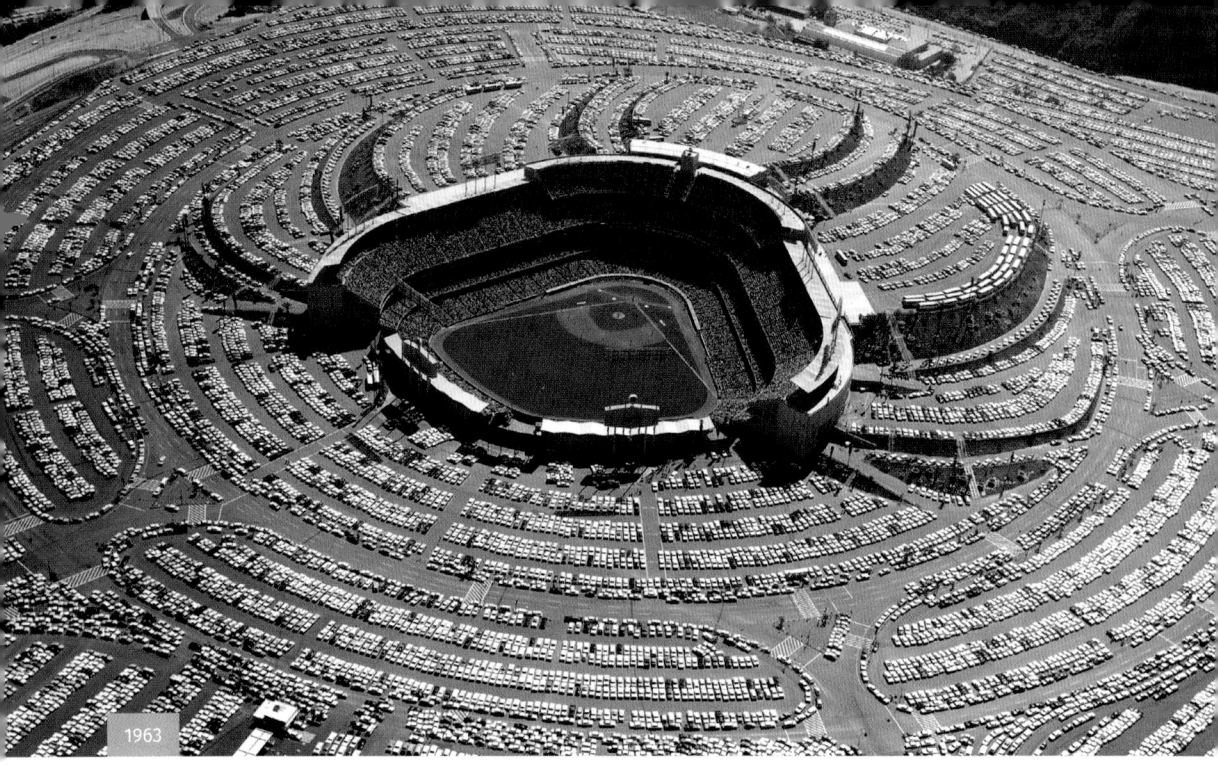

1963

DODGER STADIUM
Chavez Ravine was cleared for the Dodgers' new stadium

ABOVE: In the 1940s, Chavez Ravine was a poor, mostly Mexican American community in Sulfir Canyon. Named for Julian Chavez, a nineteenth-century city councilman, the canyon was home to mainly Hispanic families. The Los Angeles City Housing Authority earmarked Chavez Ravine's 300-plus acres as a prime location for redevelopment. In July 1950, all residents of Chavez Ravine received letters from the city telling them that they would have to sell their homes. Construction of Dodger Stadium began nine years later, and the Los Angeles Dodgers played their first game in Chavez Ravine in 1962. The parking lot offers room for 16,000 cars in twenty-one terraced lots. Since its opening, Dodger Stadium has welcomed an average of 2.8 million fans per season.

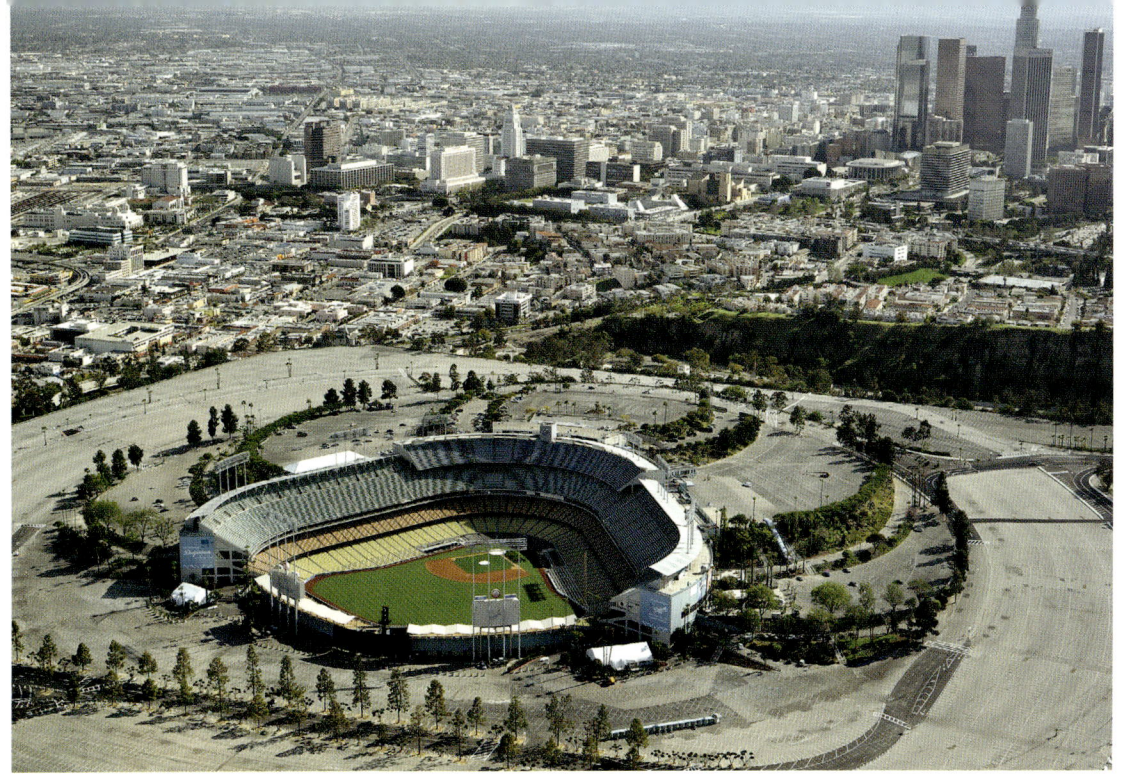

ABOVE: The 1978 season saw Dodger Stadium become the first ballpark to host more than three million fans in a season. Pope John Paul II celebrated Mass at Dodger Stadium on September 16, 1987. Entertainers from around the world have performed here, including the Rolling Stones, the Beatles, the Bee Gees, Michael Jackson, U2, and Bruce Springsteen. After the 1995 season, a new turf known as Prescription Athletic Turf was installed. It uses state-of-the-art technology to manage field moisture through controlled drainage and irrigation. By the 2000 season, the Dodgers had added new field-level seats down the foul lines and a new expanded dugout section, among other improvements. In 2003 a new scoreboard and a "DodgerVision" video board were added. After the 2005 season, all the seats within the primary seating bowl were replaced with seats that returned the stadium's look to its original 1962 color palette of yellow, light orange, turquoise, and sky blue. A statue of Jackie Robinson was unveiled April 15, 2017, along with new memorabilia displays and a gallery next to the Vin Scully Press Box.

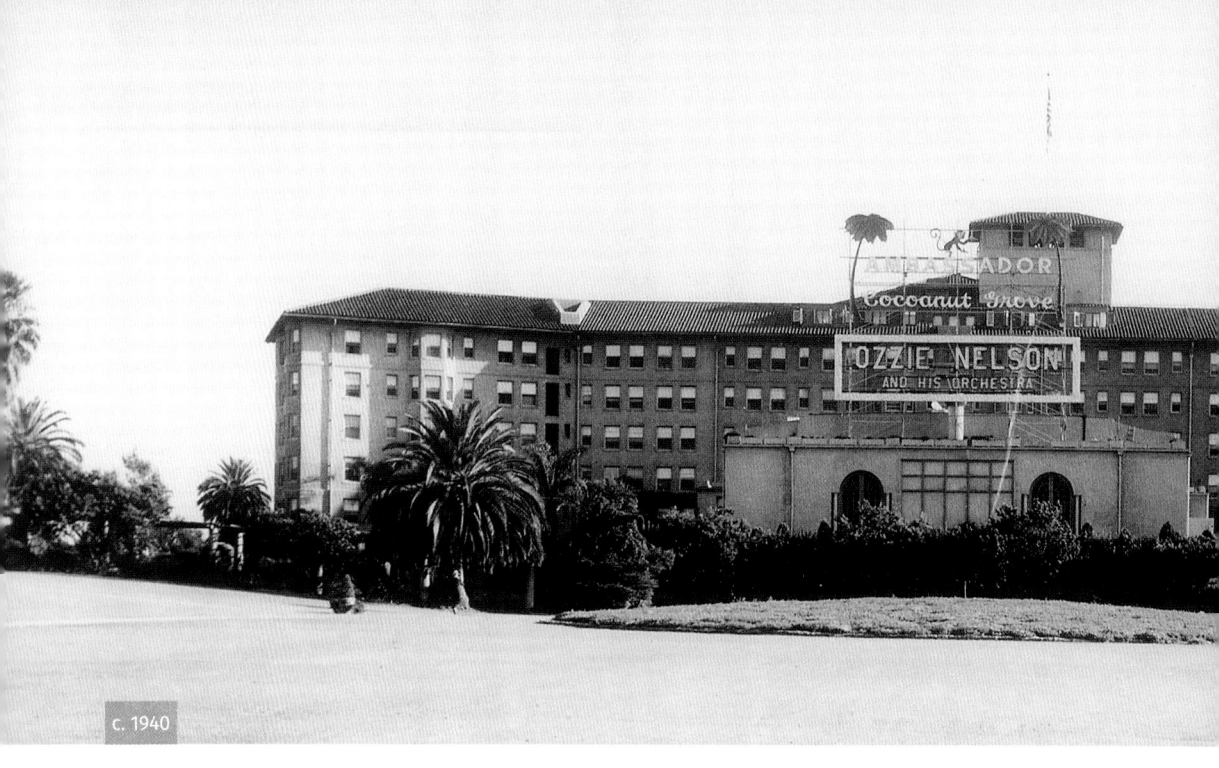

c. 1940

AMBASSADOR HOTEL

When Hollywood was in its heyday, the Ambassador was swinging

ABOVE: When the sprawling 400-room, Italian-style Ambassador Hotel opened on Wilshire Boulevard in 1921, it quickly became the place to be seen. By April 21, the Grand Ballroom had been converted into a nightclub that became world famous: Cocoanut Grove, otherwise known as the "Playground to the Stars." Guests enjoyed a tropical grove

of several hundred fake palm trees (left over from the filming of Rudolph Valentino's *The Sheik*) with fake monkeys climbing them. The tables and chairs were bamboo and wicker. This was the height of exotic glamour in the 1920s, and the stars lined up to attend and play. Charlie Chaplin entertained, Howard Hughes danced the rumba, Judy

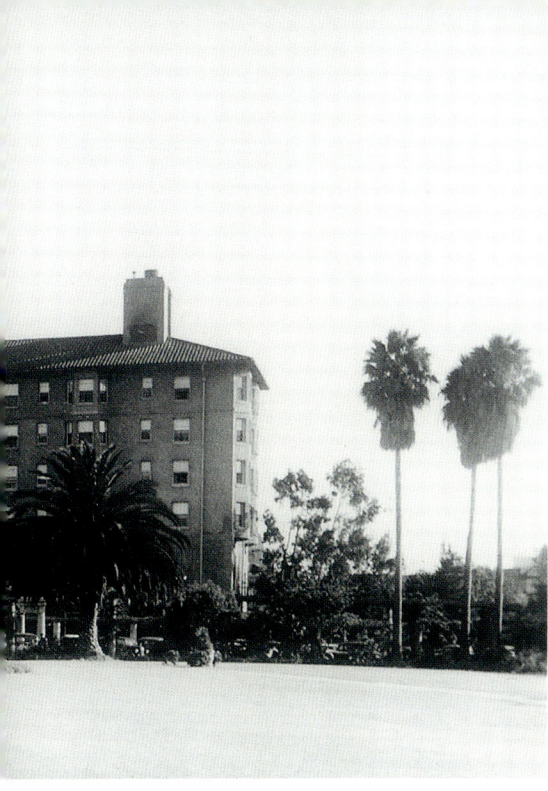

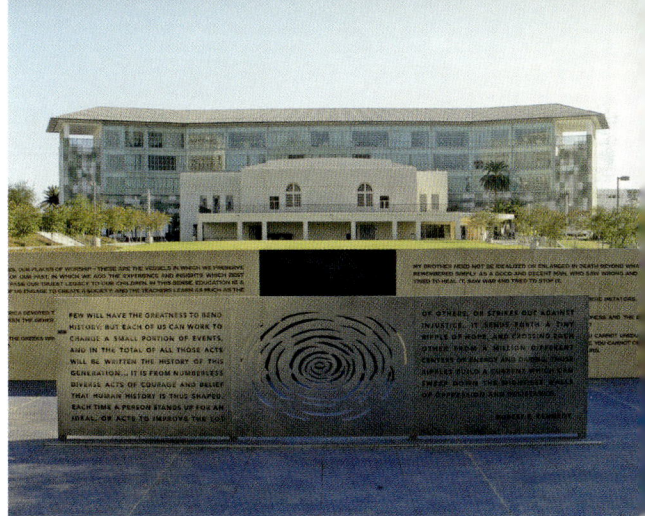

Garland sang, and Joan Crawford and Carole Lombard were said to have competed for dance trophies here. Pola Negri would walk her pet cheetah on the manicured grounds of the hotel. During the 1930s, six Academy Awards ceremonies and the first Golden Globe Awards dinner were held at the Cocoanut Grove.

ABOVE: Having just secured the California Democratic presidential primary on June 5, 1968, Senator Robert F. Kennedy was assassinated as he passed through the kitchen area of the hotel by Palestinian gunman Sirhan Sirhan. The tragedy helped accelerate the hotel's demise, along with the slide of the neighborhood. Despite a mid-1970s renovation overseen by Sammy Davis Jr. the hotel was closed in 1989. It was used as a backdrop to many films as it slowly declined over the next twenty years. It featured in *Pretty Woman*, *L.A. Story*, *The Wedding Singer*, *Apollo 13*, *Beaches*, *Catch Me If You Can*, *The Mask*, *Forrest Gump*, and *Fear and Loathing in Las Vegas*. Perhaps the greatest memorial to the Ambassador Hotel was the movie *The Thirteenth Floor*, which transformed it back to 1937 Los Angeles. From 2004 to 2005, it became the subject of a legal tussle between the Los Angeles Unified School District, which wanted to build a school on the site, and preservationists who wanted the hotel restored. The Robert F. Kennedy Community Schools were eventually built on the site and opened in 2009 and 2010.

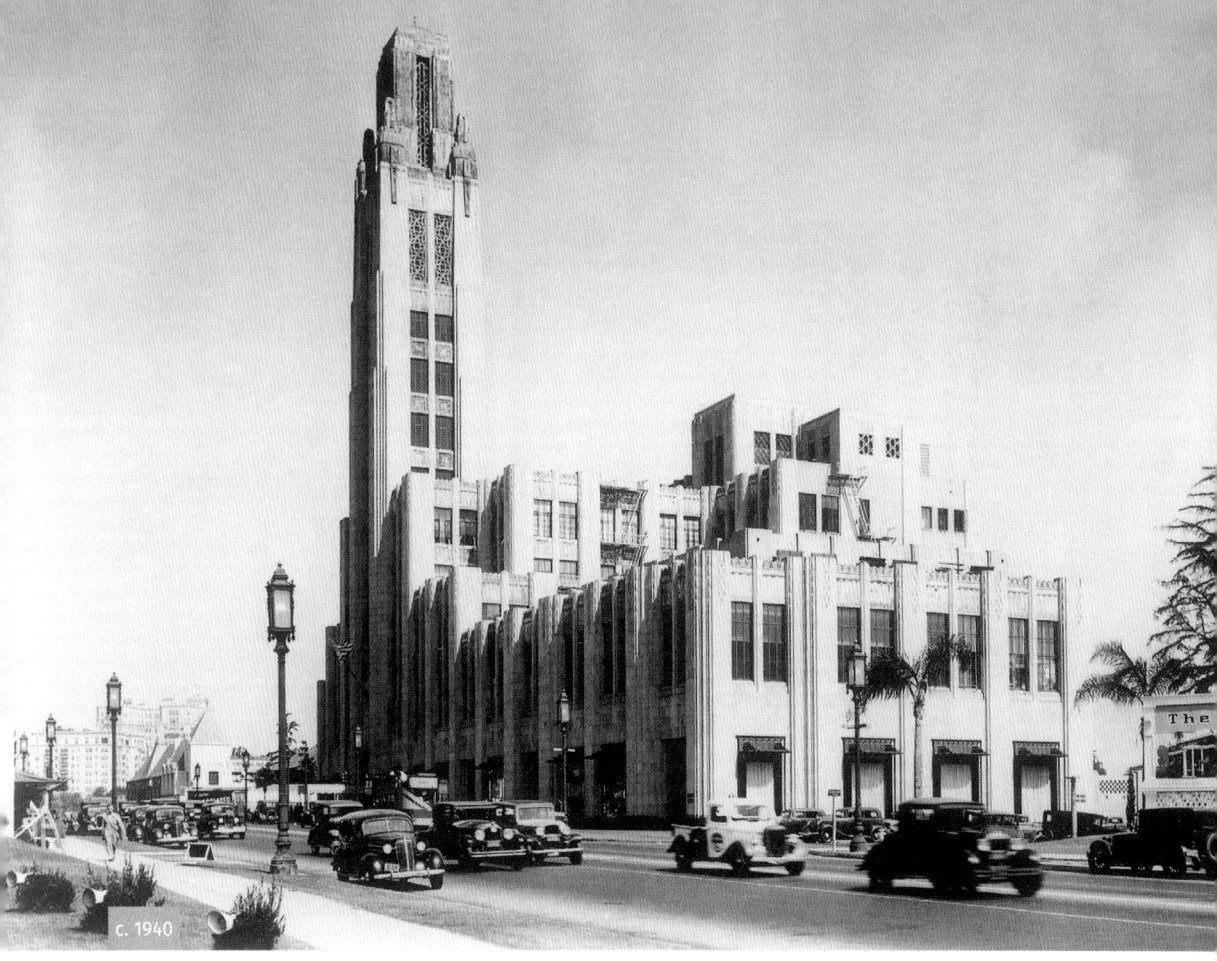

c. 1940

BULLOCKS WILSHIRE

The Art Deco department store was beautifully preserved by the Southwestern University

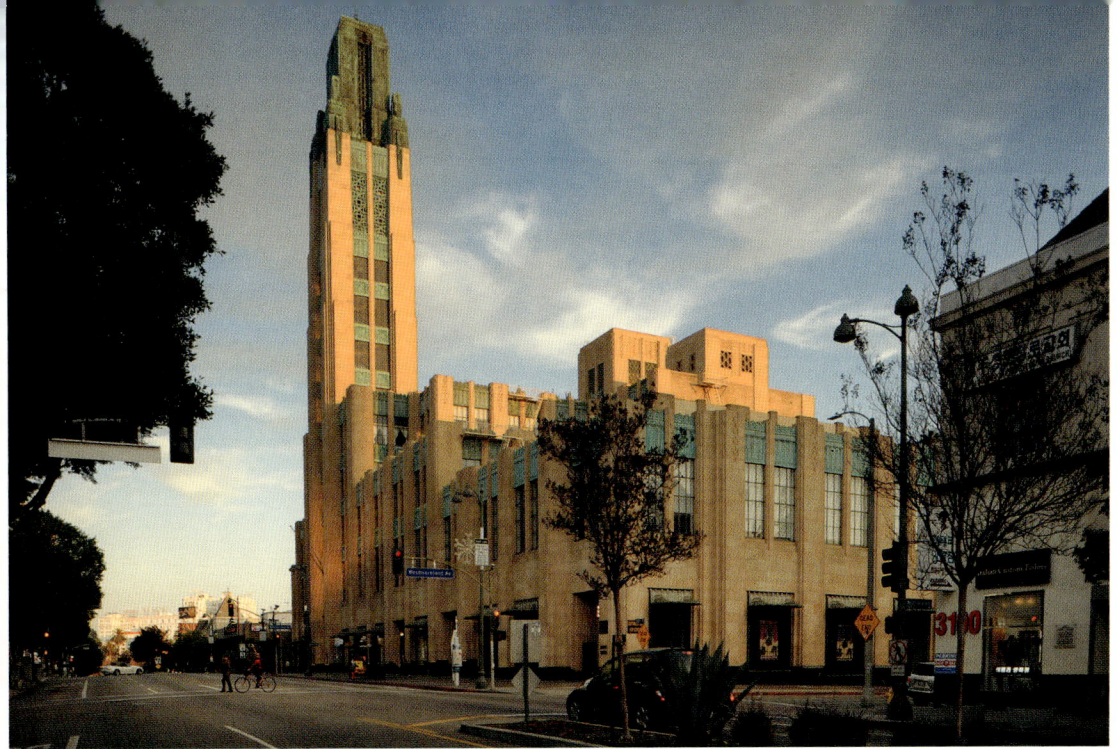

LEFT: Inspired by new designs at the Paris Exposition, John Bullock—along with John and Donald Parkinson—created the magnificent Art Deco Bullocks Wilshire department store building in 1929 as a mecca for well-heeled shoppers. With its distinctive copper-clad tower and glazed terra-cotta tile, the main entrance was at the rear, complete with uniformed parking valets. Greta Garbo, Marlene Dietrich, John Wayne, Clark Gable, and Barbara Stanwyck were devoted patrons. Angela Lansbury worked in the store as a teenager and, many years later, came back to film an episode of *Murder, She Wrote*.

ABOVE: Shoppers moved west as new malls sprang up, and Bullocks Wilshire fell into decline. But the top-floor tearoom, famous for its coconut cream pie and fashion shows, was popular to the end. When the store closed in 1996, it was bought by the Southwestern University School of Law and restored to its former splendor. Southwestern won awards for the preservation and restoration. The famous tearoom is now a cafeteria and study hall. It is open to the public during summer break only, on the school's annual Tea and Tour Day. The building continues to be used for filming when school is not in session.

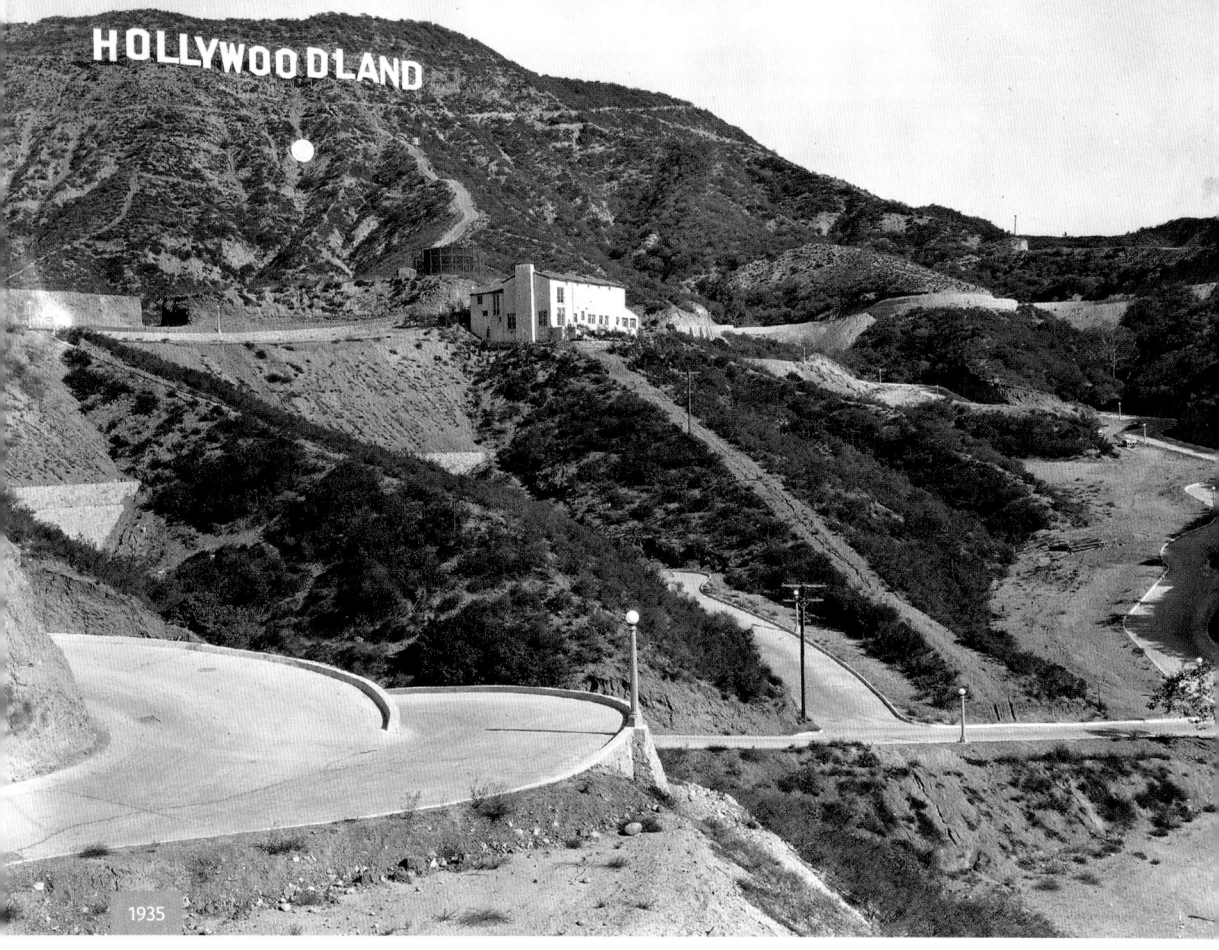

1935

THE HOLLYWOOD SIGN

The sign fell rapidly into decline once maintenance ceased in 1939

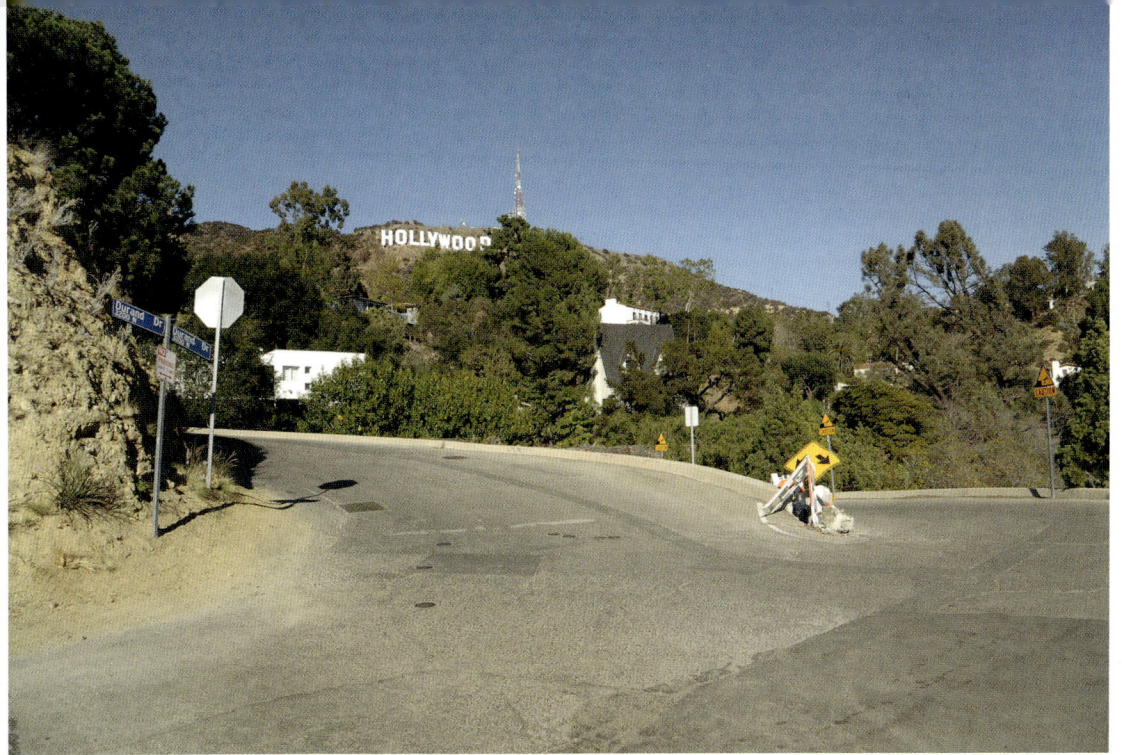

LEFT: By the time of this photo in 1935, the Hollywoodland sign had been gracing Mount Lee for thirteen years. The original Hollywoodland sign was erected in 1923 by developers as an advertising gimmick. The letters were fifty feet tall and thirty feet wide, and were made of white-painted metal squares studded with 4,000 twenty-watt bulbs; the sign cost $21,000 to build. The sign was maintained by a caretaker who lived in a small house behind the sign. A thirty-five-foot, white-painted metal circle (seen as a small white dot from miles away) was put 200 feet below as an eye-catcher.

ABOVE: In 1939 maintenance ceased and 4,000 lightbulbs were stolen by vandals. Developers donated the sign to the city, which decided to restore just the "Hollywood" without the "land." During the 1960s, the Hollywood Kiwanis Club raised enough money to repair the sign. But soon after Kiwanis spent the last of their funds, one of the Os crumbled. In 1978 Alice Cooper spearheaded a public campaign to restore the landmark when he donated $27,000 to replace the missing O. Hugh Hefner and Andy Williams were among other celebrities donating money to save the sign.

BEACHWOOD GATES

The entrance to Hollywoodland

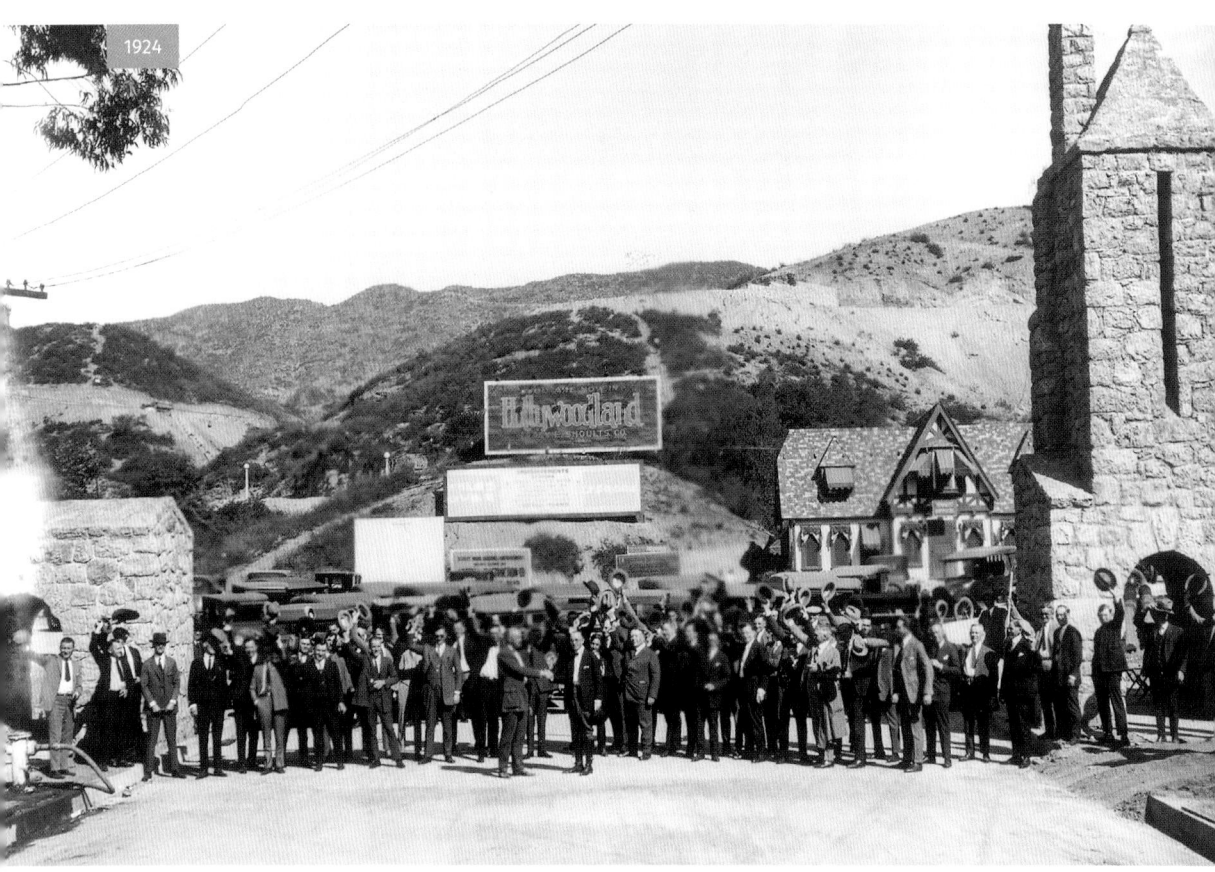

1924

LEFT: Developer Albert Beach paved the way to the Hollywood Hills with a road he named after himself: Beachwood Drive. In 1923 the director of Pacific Electric Railway, M. H. Sherman, joined Harry Chandler, Tracey Shoults, and developer S. H. Woodruff and formed the Hollywoodland Tract Realty with an office at the Hollywoodland entrance. They built two stone towers on either side and planned to gate the community with a guard on night duty—but the gate and the guard never materialized.

BELOW: Relatively unchanged, Beachwood Village today is home to many writers, actors, and artists. Underneath the Hollywood sign, Beachwood Canyon now stops at the Sunset Ranch, where cowboys, actors, and horse lovers alike stable their horses and ride through the Hollywood Hills at sunset. The Village Café is a family café where stars go for breakfast with the rest of the world. Next to the café are a supermarket and a small antiques store. This area became famous after *The Invasion of the Body Snatchers*.

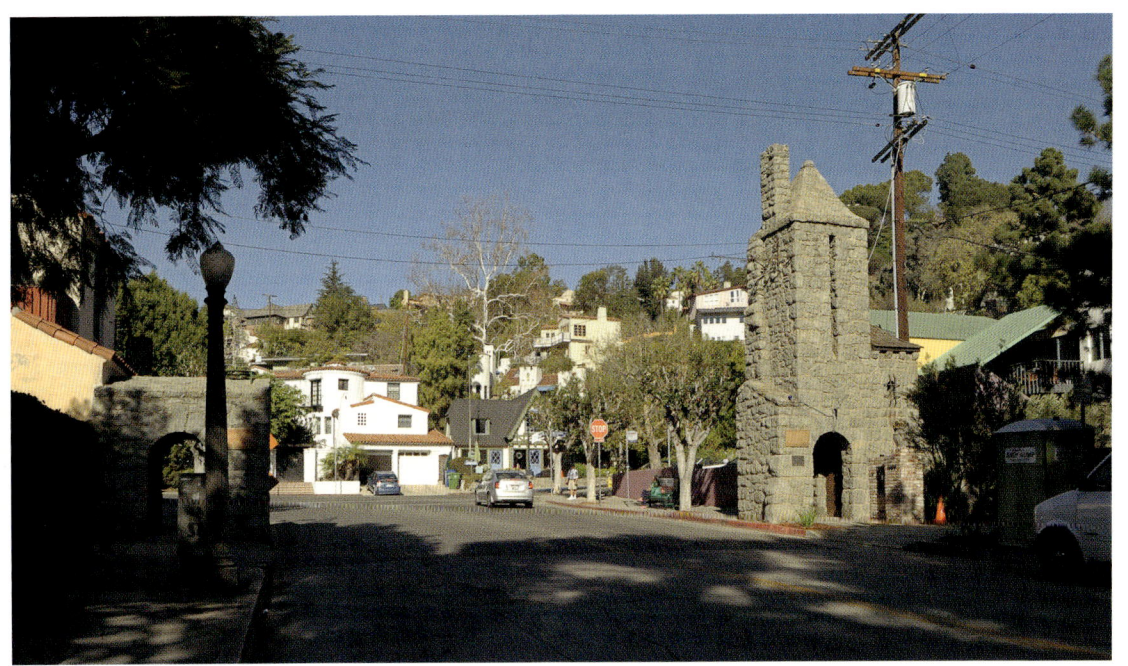

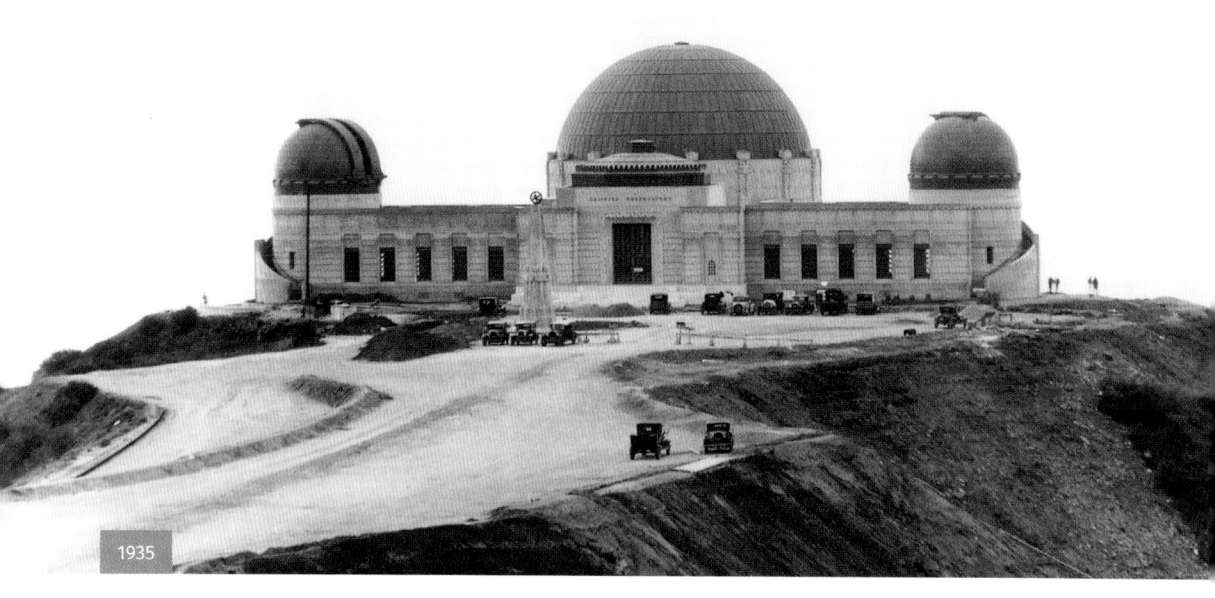

1935

GRIFFITH OBSERVATORY
The Welsh-born benefactor never got to see his great gift to the city

ABOVE: Colonel Griffith J. Griffith donated 3,015 acres to the City of Los Angeles in 1896 for the creation of a "great park." After making a fortune in Mexican silver mines, Griffith had invested in Southern California real estate. He visited the world's largest telescope at the new research observatory established at Mount Wilson, north of Los Angeles, in 1904. The telescope so impressed him that, in 1912, Griffith offered Los Angeles $100,000 to build an observatory atop Mount Hollywood. Griffith's plan included an astronomical telescope open to free viewing, a hall of science, and an auditorium. The Griffith Observatory has graced the south-facing slope of Mount Hollywood in Griffith Park since 1935, when these photographs were taken. Colonel Griffith died in 1919, fourteen years before construction on the site began.

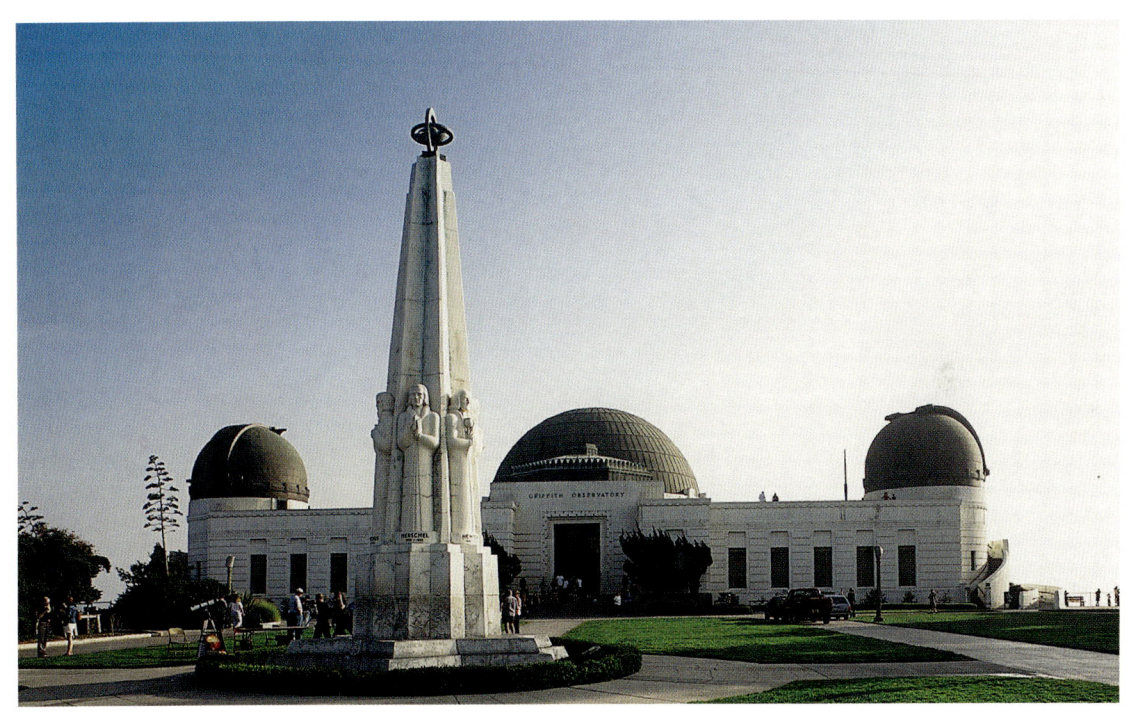

ABOVE: During World War II, a large air-raid siren was set up next door and squadrons of naval aviators learned to navigate by the stars in the planetarium. Cosmologist Fritz Zwicky, who discovered dark matter, neutron stars, and supernovas, used the telescope for his research several times in the 1950s. The 1980s and 1990s brought unprecedented crowds to the Griffith Observatory, with attendance reaching an annual average of about two million visitors. The copper domes of the observatory were shined up to a "penny finish" in 1984, a year before the celebration of the building's fiftieth anniversary. Major astronomical events such as Halley's Comet in 1986 and the impact of the Shoemaker-Levy 9 Comet with Jupiter in 1994 raised the observatory's profile even further. The observatory was closed from 2002 until November 2006 for a $93 million renovation and expansion. Building under ground, new exhibits, the Wolfgang Puck restaurant and the Leonard Nimoy Event Horizon Theatre were created.

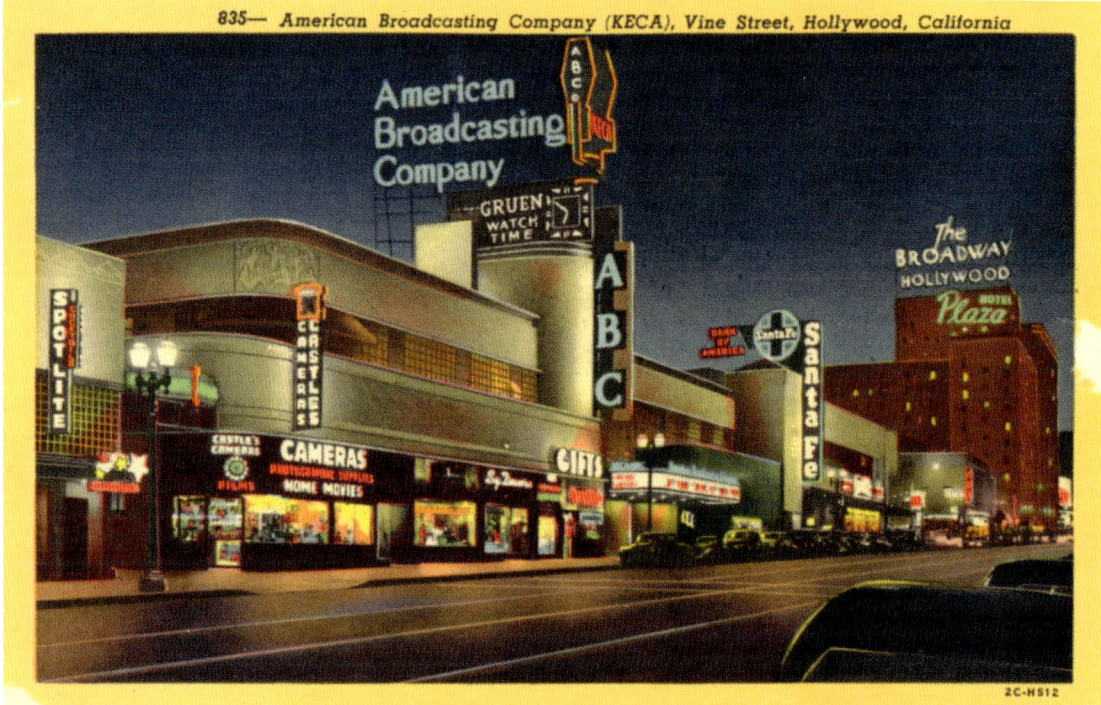

835— American Broadcasting Company (KECA), Vine Street, Hollywood, California

VINE STREET

The Hollywood Recreation Center has had many occupants through the years

ABOVE: In the 1920s, the motion picture and radio industries were blossoming and gravitated toward the office buildings newly constructed at Hollywood Boulevard and Vine Street. Just south of the intersection was the Hollywood Recreation Center, a 1935 Streamline Moderne building that originally housed bowling lanes, which Tom Breneman and Sammy Davis Jr. bought and leased to ABC Radio for their national broadcasts. Further along the street the Broadway sign sits atop what was originally the B. H. Dyas Specialty Emporium. Built in 1927 on the southwest corner of Hollywood and Vine, across from the Taft building, the Broadway Department Store took it over in 1931. Also south of Hollywood Boulevard, the Vine Street Theatre was built in 1926. During the 1930s this was home to CBS Radio Playhouse, broadcasting the Lux Radio Theatre, featuring stars such as William Holden, Gloria Swanson, and George Raft.

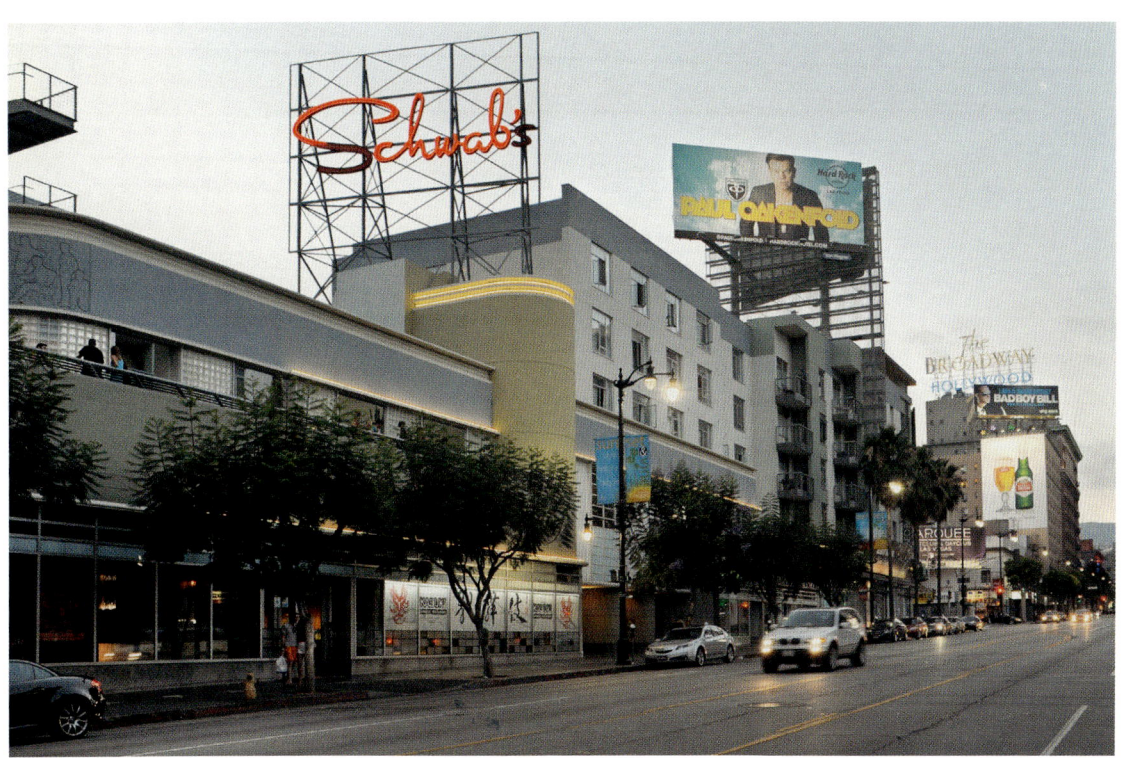

ABOVE: Merv Griffin took over the ABC building at the end of the 1970s and renamed it the Celebrity Theater, home to the Merv Griffin Show. After the show ended its run, the building was vacated in 1993 and it became the home of transients who destroyed many of the historical details of the building, which suffered two suspicious fires. It was taken in hand and remodeled in 2004, with Hollywood Heritage keeping a close eye on the retention of the Streamline Moderne facade. The Broadway Department Store finally closed its doors in 1982, and although the historic sign remains, the building has been converted to apartments. After subsequent incarnations, the old CBS Radio Playhouse has become the Ricardo Montalbán Theatre.

EGYPTIAN THEATRE

Sid Grauman's first Hollywood movie house

1922

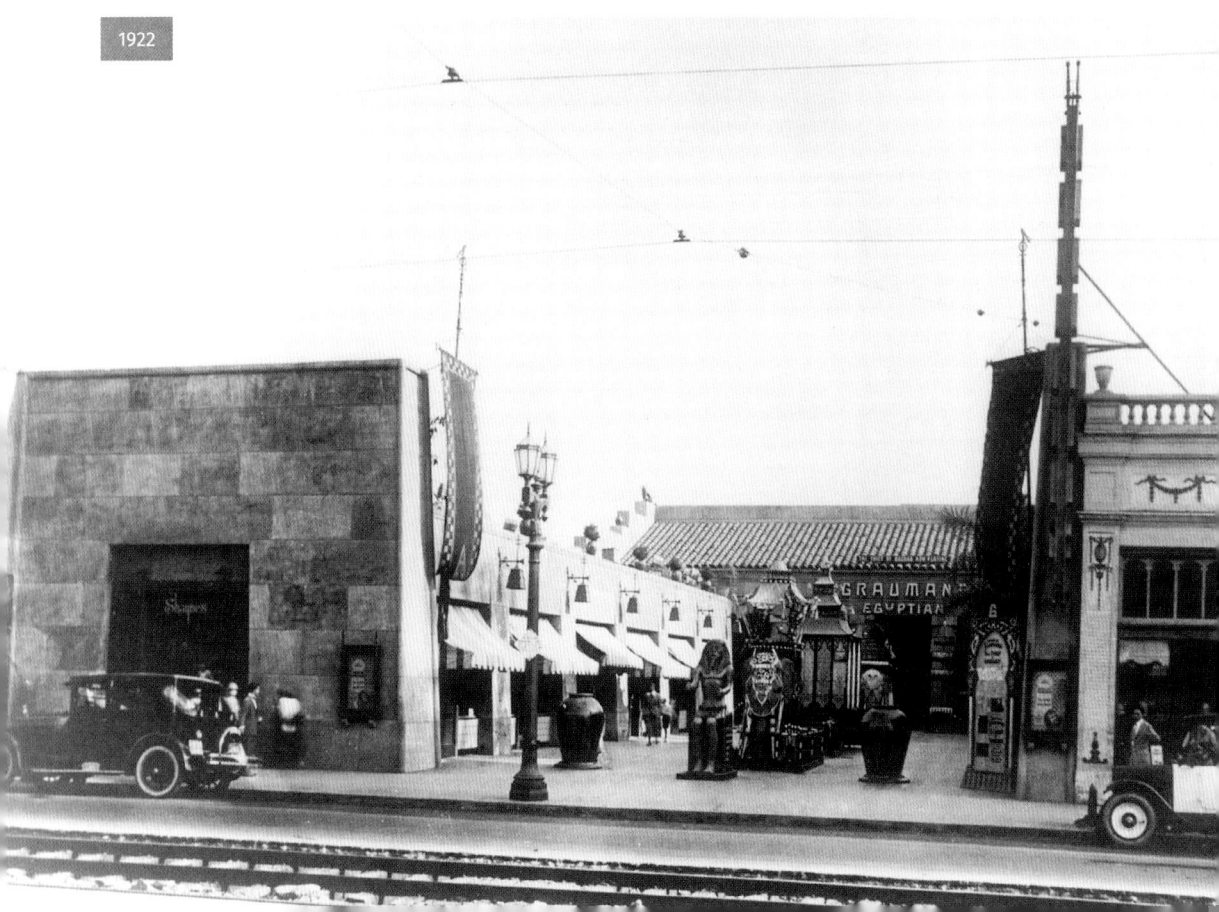

LEFT: The Egyptian Theatre, inspired by the discovery of King Tut's tomb, was the first Grauman theater in Hollywood, opening in 1922 with the premiere of Douglas Fairbanks's *Robin Hood*. It was the first theater to have a forecourt, and Grauman chose film props from the current movie for display. On the roof, an actor in an Egyptian costume marched back and forth calling out the start to each performance. For Cecil B. DeMille's *The Ten Commandments* premiere in 1923, Grauman had over a hundred costumed performers on parade.

BELOW: The Egyptian Theatre closed in 1992, and reopened in 1998 following a $15 million refurbishment. American Cinematheque (a nonprofit arts organization) bought it from the city for one dollar promising to restore it to its former grandeur as a movie theater and add programs on filmmaking past and present. The historic ceilings and the 1922 theater organ were also repaired. Sharon Stone narrates the in-house documentary, "Forever Hollywood," and celebrity panels and historic tours are interspersed with screenings of old movies. The adjacent Pig 'n' Whistle Café (famous for its sundaes since 1927) was also restored.

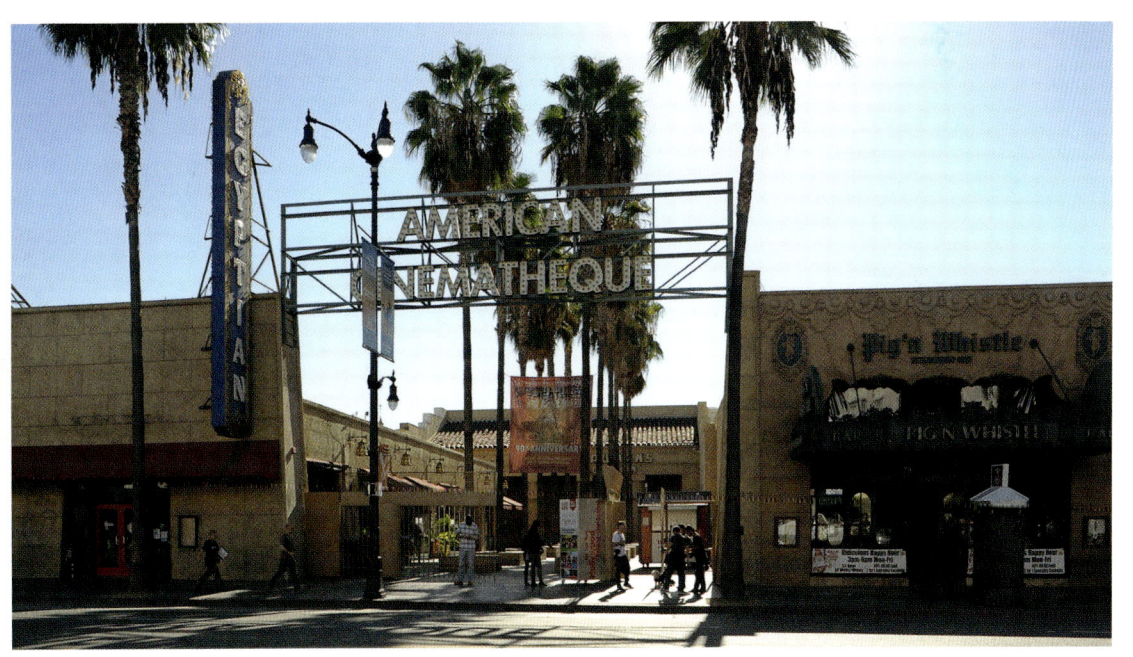

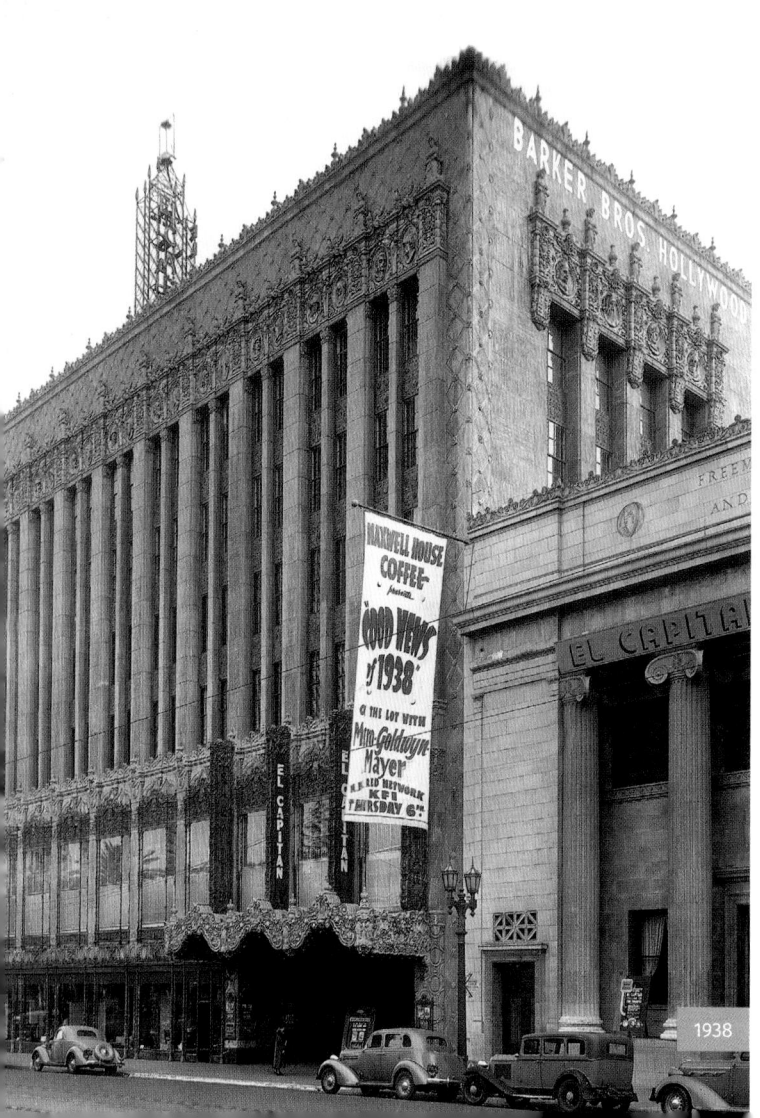

1938

EL CAPITAN THEATRE

The Walt Disney Company has returned the El Capitan to its former glory

LEFT: Real estate developer Charles Toberman (often dubbed the "Father of Hollywood") envisioned a thriving Hollywood theater district. Together with Sid Grauman, he built the Egyptian, El Capitan, and Chinese Theatres. The El Capitan opened on May 3, 1926, with *Charlot's Revue*, starring Jack Buchanan and Gertrude Lawrence. In the next decade, over 120 live plays were produced with luminaries such as Clark Gable and Joan Fontaine treading the boards. After the Great Depression, audiences declined and the El Capitan began to screen movies instead. It closed shortly after Orson Welles's *Citizen Kane* premiered there in 1941.

RIGHT: After a full conversion to a cinema, the theater reopened in 1942 as the Paramount. After the 1960s, the Paramount changed hands often. In 1989 the Walt Disney Company took over, restoring this historical gem to its original Spanish Colonial and East Indian splendor, adding a giant Wurlitzer theater organ and returning to its original name. Today, Disney films premiere at the El Capitan, along with live stage shows. Using the neighboring Masonic Temple (frequented by Charlie Chaplin, Bob Hope, and Cecil B. DeMille in its day), Disney has added attractions such as the Disney Monsters Fun Palace, Toy Story, a soda fountain, and the studio store. *The Jimmy Kimmel Show* tapes here. El Capitan was used as the Muppets Theatre in *The Muppets* (2011). A special "sing-along" screening of the film *Mary Poppins* was held here in 2014.

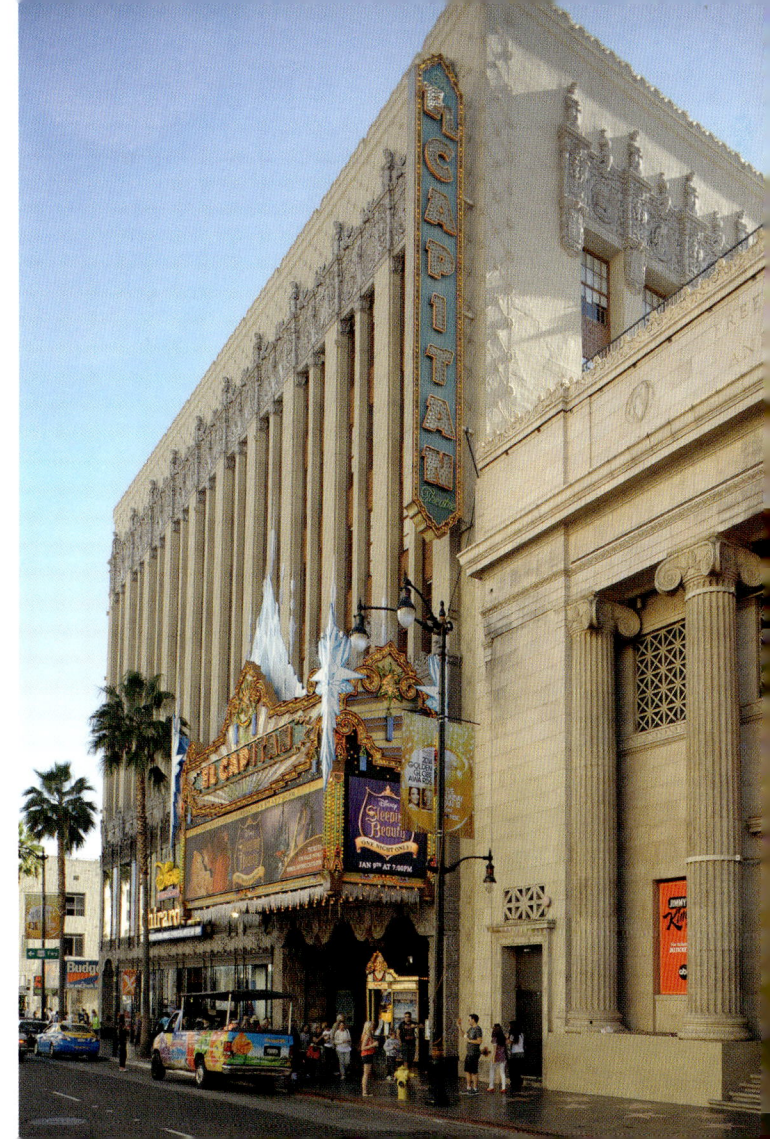

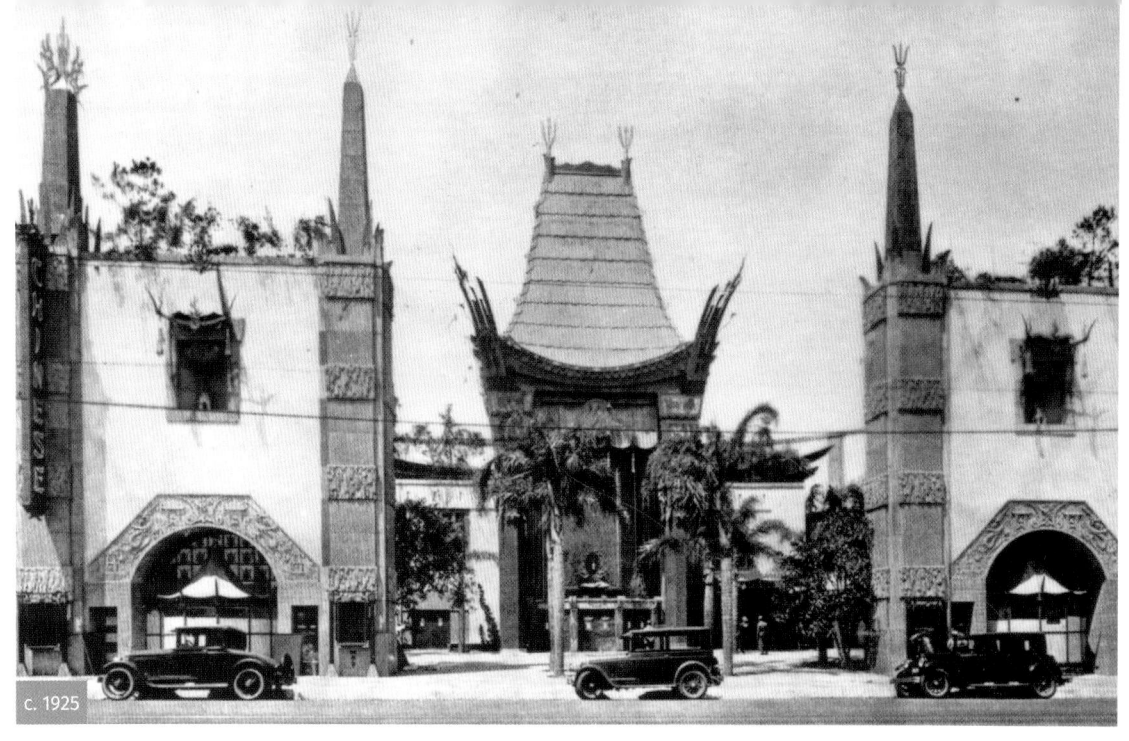

c. 1925

GRAUMAN'S CHINESE THEATRE

Sid Grauman's happy knack with publicity helped create the world's most famous cinema

ABOVE: Grauman's Chinese Theatre opened on May 18, 1927. It was commissioned following the success of the nearby Grauman's Egyptian Theatre, which opened five years earlier. At a cost of $2 million, the theater was to be Sid Grauman's masterpiece. It opened with the premiere of Cecil B. DeMille's film *The King of Kings*. The opening attracted thousands of people, and the crowd became unruly as fans tried to catch a glimpse of arriving movie stars and celebrities. Grauman spared no expense on the theater's decor. He imported temple bells, pagodas, and other artifacts from China with special permission from the U.S. government. The first footprint ceremony took place on April 30, 1927, when Mary Pickford and Douglas Fairbanks pressed their feet into squares of wet cement. Norma Talmadge had accidentally stepped into wet cement on the forecourt, giving showman Sid Grauman his famous idea.

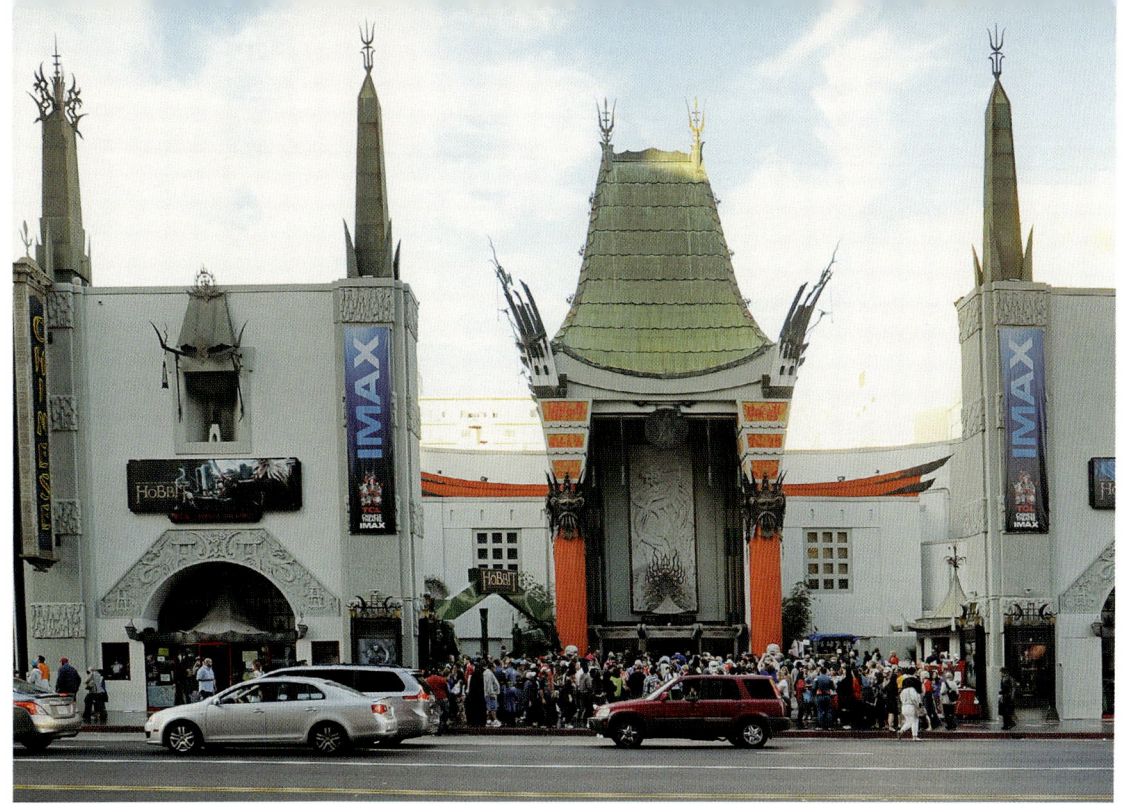

ABOVE: Known for its gala premieres, the Chinese Theatre had over 10,000 spectators for the 1939 opening of *The Wizard of Oz*. Ever since that sidewalk-shaping event in 1927, the stars of yesterday and today have left their footprints in the sidewalks near the theater. Little has changed at 6925 Hollywood Boulevard. Grauman's Chinese Theatre remains a much sought-after venue for premieres, and more than four million tourists visit its cement handprints and footprints in the forecourt every year. The theater is steeped in Hollywood tradition. The two original giant "Heaven Dogs" brought from China still guard the theater's entryway. Following the Northridge earthquake of 1994, an extensive retrofit was implemented. In 2013 the owners teamed with Chinese electronics manufacturer TCL (The Creative Life) in a 10-year, multimillion-dollar partnership that included naming rights. And so it is now officially known as the TCL Chinese Theatre until 2023.

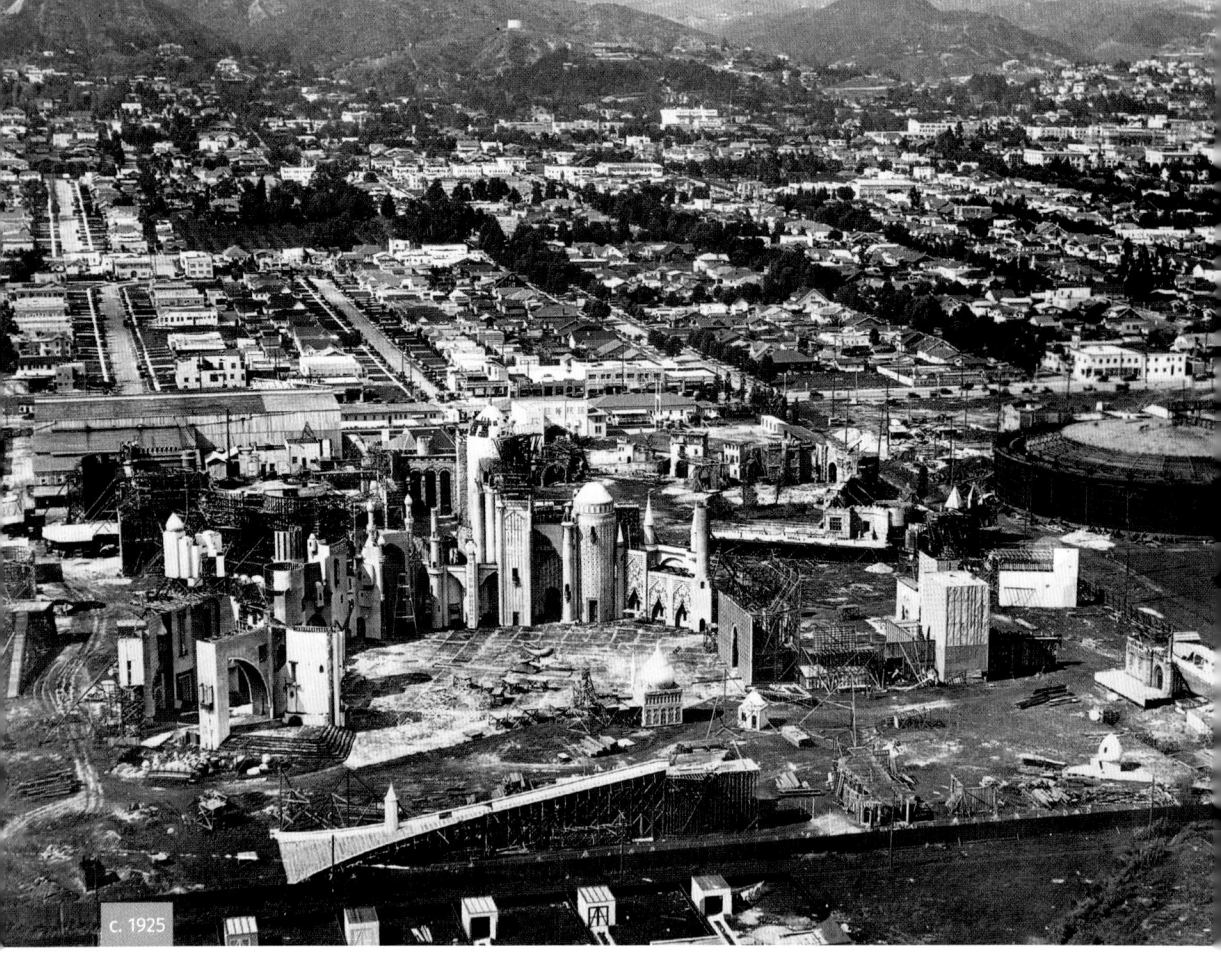

c. 1925

PICKFORD STUDIOS

Jesse Hampton's original film studio is still a place where movies are made

64

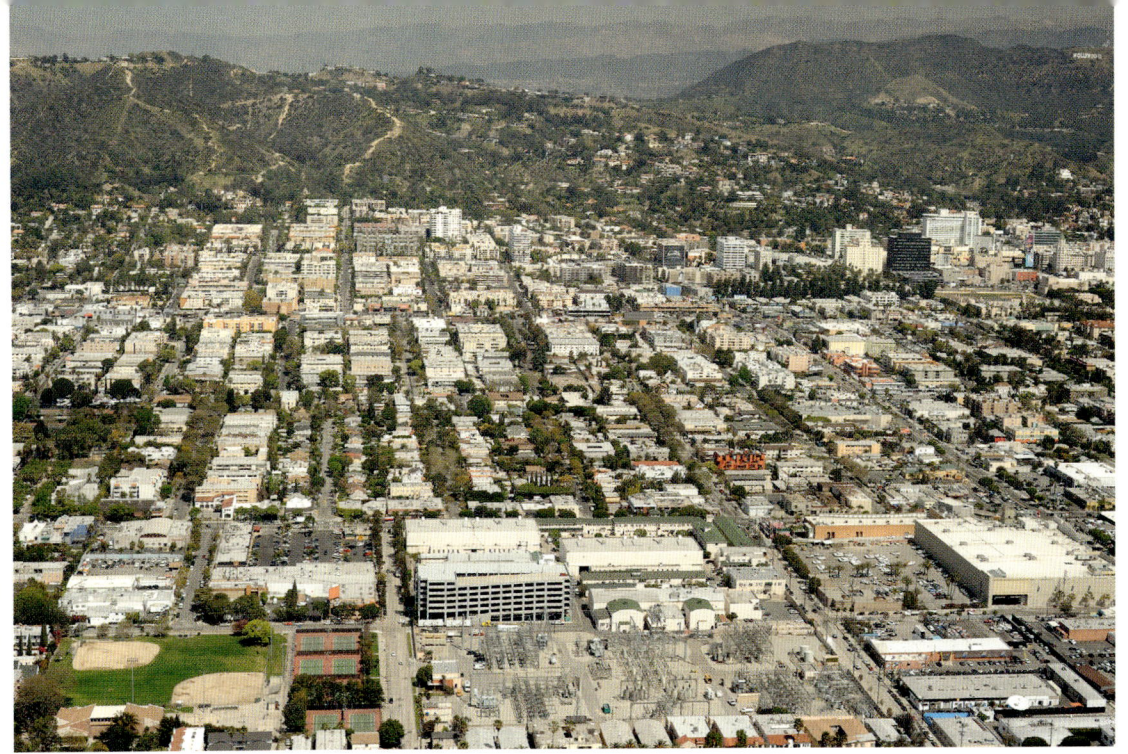

LEFT: The set for the movie *The Thief of Baghdad* helps date this photograph to after 1924. This studio began as Hampton Studios when Jesse D. Hampton opened it to house his growing production company around 1918. Once Hampton moved out, the "first couple" of Hollywood, Mary Pickford and Douglas Fairbanks, purchased the studio. In 1919, along with Charlie Chaplin and D. W. Griffith, Pickford and Fairbanks founded United Artists and used this studio as HQ. The studio released the classics *Robin Hood* and *The Thief of Baghdad*.

ABOVE: Since the days of Fairbanks and Pickford, the studio has changed hands many times. During the 1950s, United Artists partner Samuel Goldwyn took over the facility, named it after himself, and generated hits such as *West Side Story* and *Some Like It Hot*. Warner Bros. purchased the studio in the 1980s and called it Warner Hollywood. Now featuring seven soundstages, the studio continues to be active, producing mostly television series. The studio was sold again in 1999 to BA Studios, a company that rents production facilities to Warner Bros. and other firms. Today the site is simply called "the Lot."

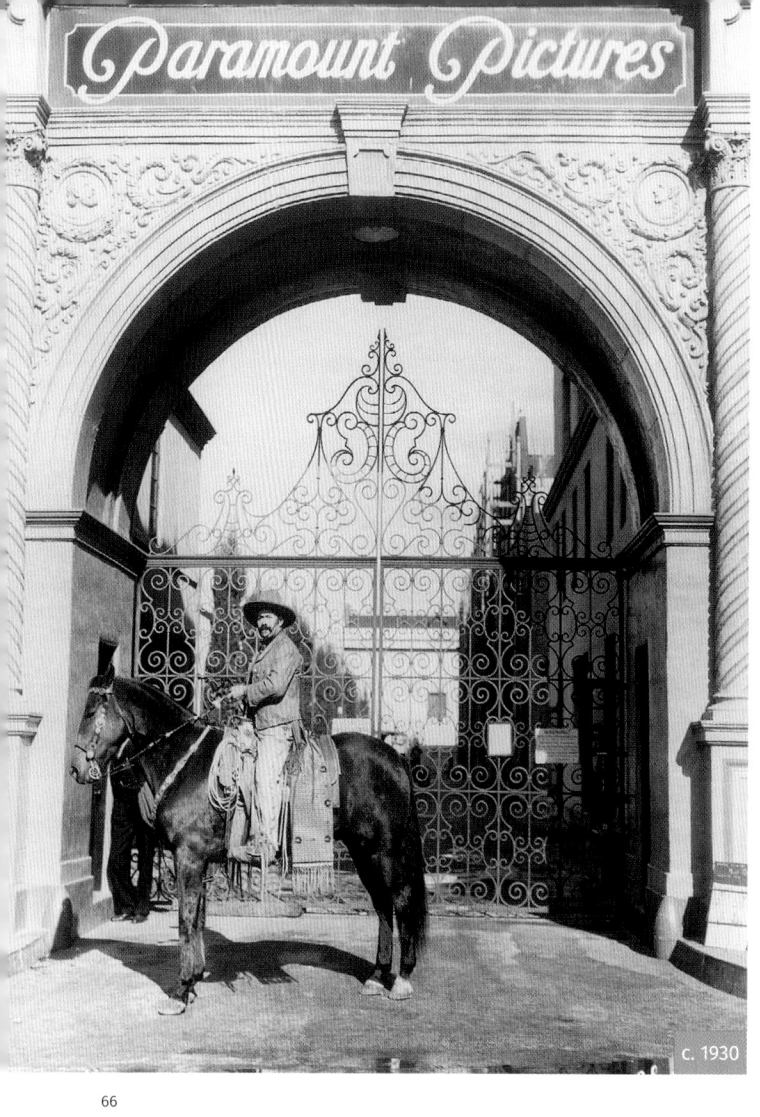

c. 1930

PARAMOUNT STUDIOS
The great Hollywood survivor

LEFT: Paramount is the only major film studio still operating in Hollywood. Famous Players-Lasky Corporation took over the 1917-built United Studios in 1926 and renamed it Paramount. Some of the biggest names in showbusiness, including Mae West, W. C. Fields, and the Marx brothers, filmed here. In 1957 Desilu Productions (of the *I Love Lucy* series) took over RKO Studios on Gower, which eventually became part of the Paramount lot. The Bronson Gate, shown here, was featured in *Sunset Boulevard*, starring William Holden and Gloria Swanson.

RIGHT: In 1966 Paramount was taken over by Gulf and Western, which also absorbed Desilu Productions. Paramount then produced *Rear Window*, *Breakfast at Tiffany's*, and *The Godfather* trilogy. Paramount Television began in 1967 with series such as *Gunsmoke* and *Happy Days*. Viacom bought the studio in 1994 for $10 billion. The Indiana Jones, *Star Trek*, *Mission: Impossible*, *Anchorman*, and Jack Reacher movies are among some of Paramount's great successes.

RIGHT: The Paramount back lot has a seascape sky in front of a large water tank that, when empty, also doubles as a parking lot. It also has a variety of New York streets it can choose from.

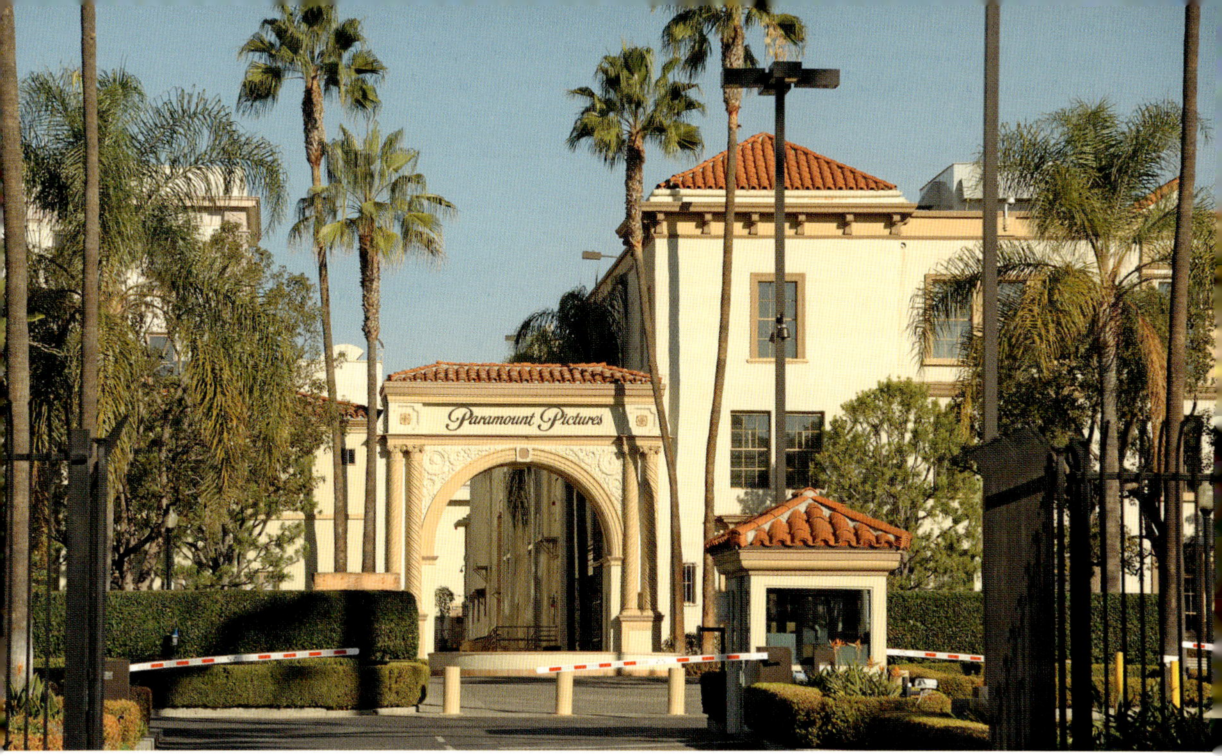

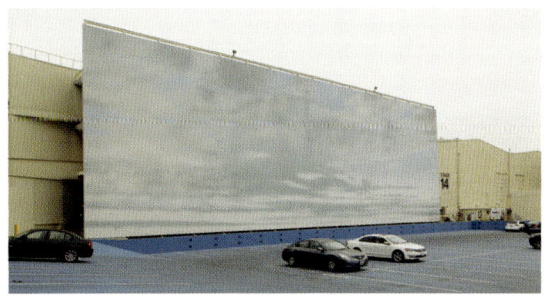

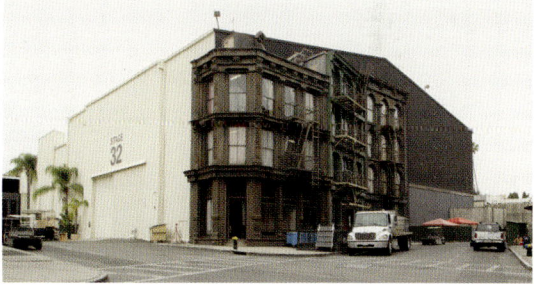

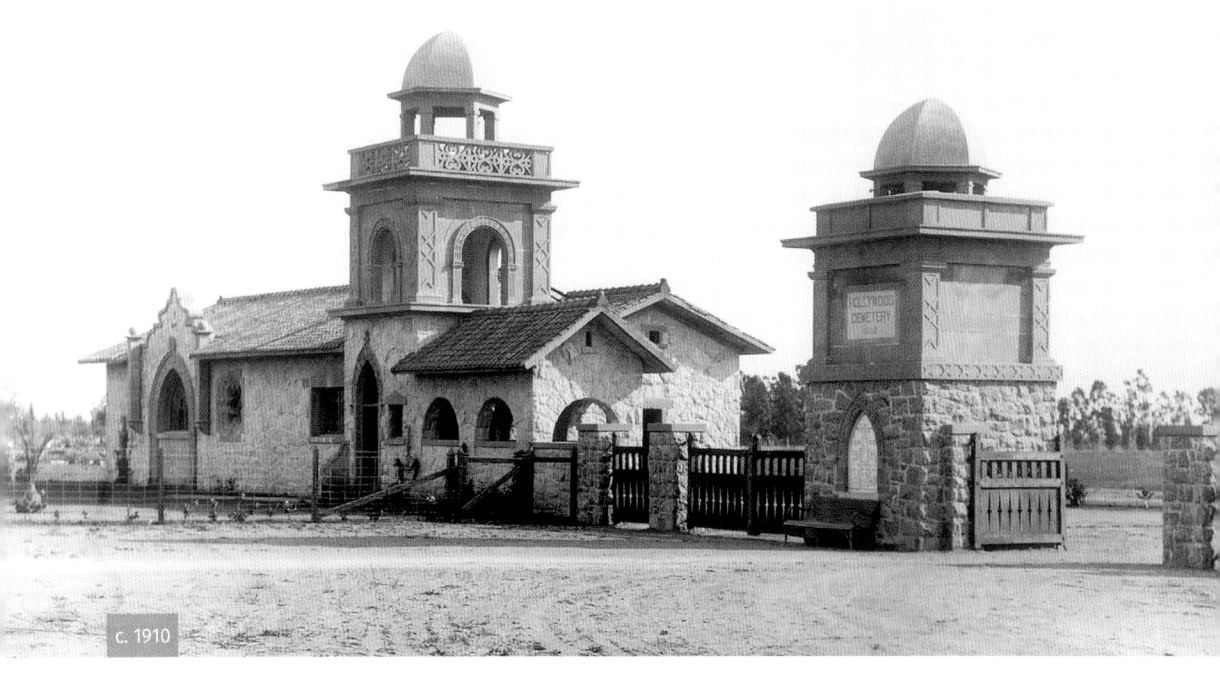

c. 1910

HOLLYWOOD MEMORIAL PARK / HOLLYWOOD FOREVER
Once again worthy of its glamorous Hollywood heritage

ABOVE: Established in 1899, the cemetery was founded by Isaac Van Nuys and was known as the Hollywood Memorial Park Cemetery. The cemetery was planned long before the movie business came to town, but today it is a *Who's Who* of old Hollywood. When Rudolph Valentino died in 1926 at the age of thirty-one, 10,000 people came to pay their respects. Mausoleums and elegant headstones in memory of stars such as Peter Finch, Jayne Mansfield, John Huston, Edward G. Robinson, Douglas Fairbanks, Cecil B. DeMille, Tyrone Power, Harrison Gray Otis, and Griffith J. Griffith are found here. Originally a hundred-acre park, the southern thirty-eight acres were sold to Paramount Studios.

68

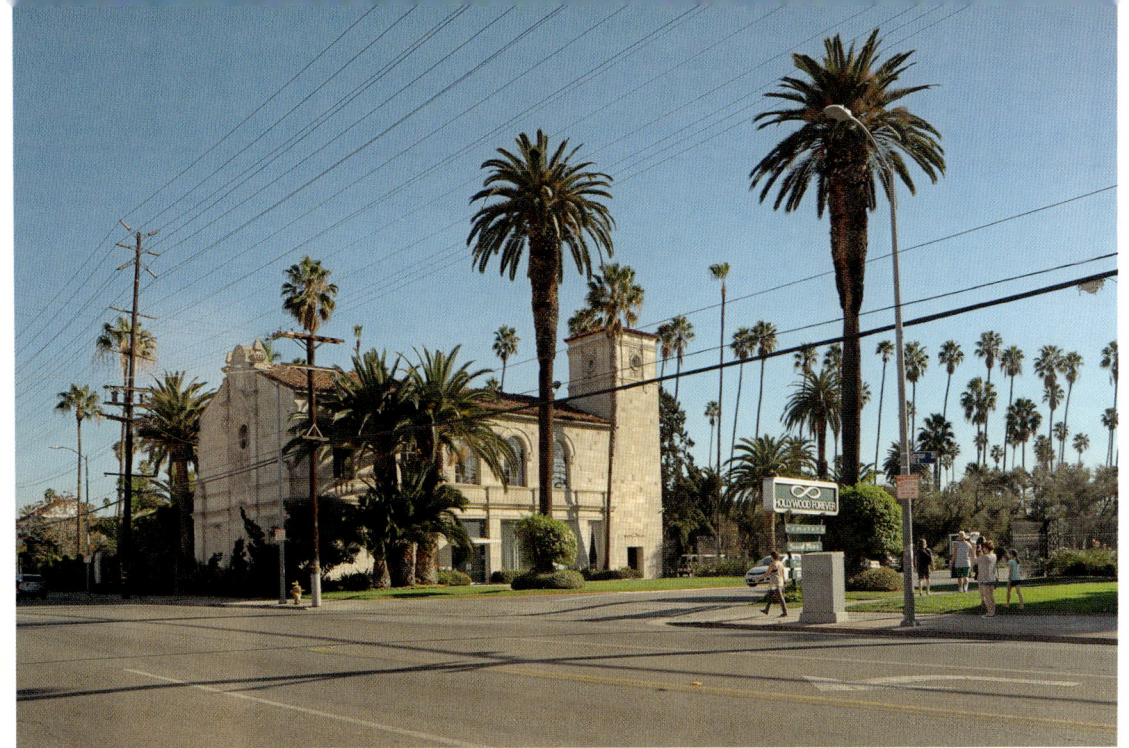

ABOVE: The cemetery was renamed Hollywood Forever when Tyler and Brent Cassity bought it for $375,000 in 1998. It had fallen into decline from the 1940s after being bought by fraudster Jules Roth, who had asset-stripped the business. The 1994 Northridge earthquake had toppled headstones and damaged roads, and maintenance and restoration was sorely needed. The Cassity family brought a new energy to a neglected cemetery park. They added a Day of the Dead celebration, weddings, and silent-movie nights in the summer with picnics and movies projected on mausoleum walls. Around 3,000 attend the regular music concerts. For families of the "residents," a Life Stories service is highly popular: either written or video memoirs are available—including Life Stories of the celebrities buried there. Actress Joan Hackett still makes people smile—her gravestone reads: "Go away, I'm sleeping." The ghost of actor Clifton Webb is said to haunt his mausoleum in the park. One of the more recent interments—Johnny Ramone in 2004—has generated his own annual tribute with contemporaries of the Ramones' guitarist putting in appearances.

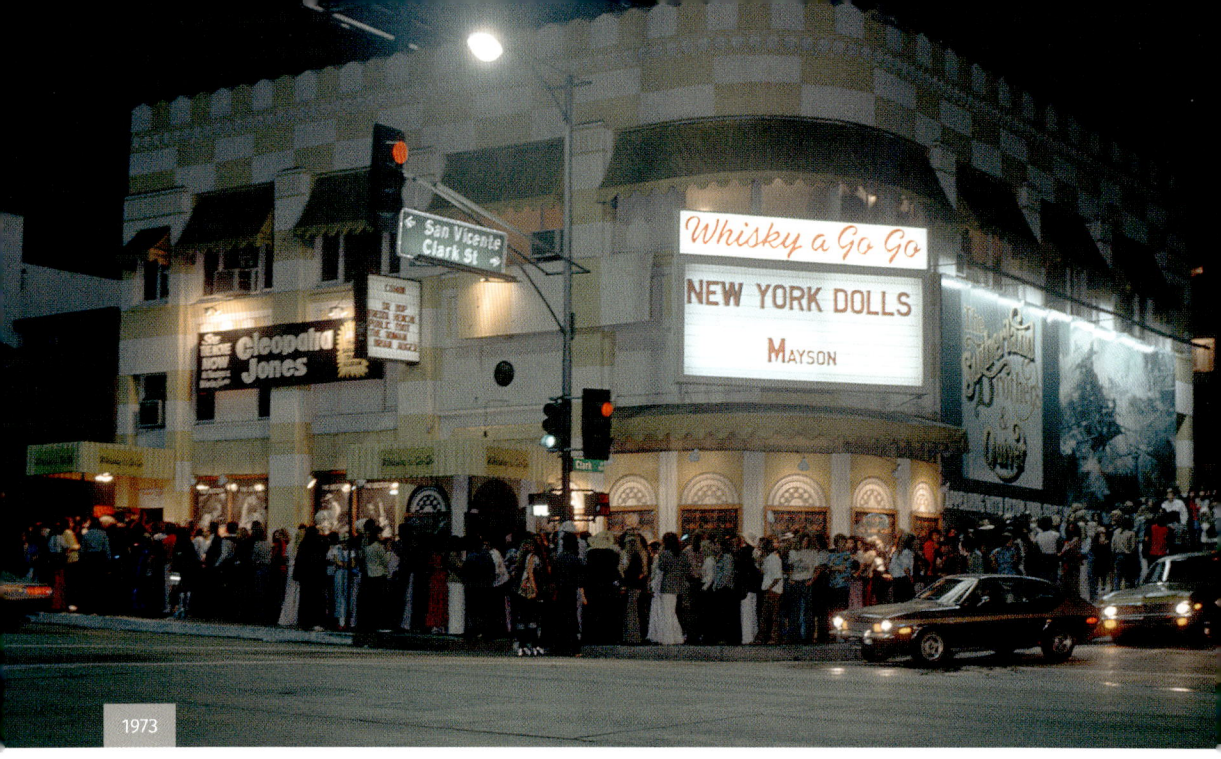

1973

WHISKY A GO GO

Where a generation of rock acts paid their dues

ABOVE: On January 15, 1964, Elmer Valentine introduced Whisky a Go Go to an unsuspecting world and changed the music scene forever. Singer-songwriter-guitarist Johnny Rivers became an instant success when he performed live at the discotheque that night. In between sets, female DJs suspended in a glass cage above the stage played music for the crowd to dance to, simply because there was not enough floor room. In the glass cage, the Go Go girls in their fringed minidresses and white boots created an indelible image. An eclectic group of bands found a home on the Sunset Strip at the Whisky, including the Byrds, Alice Cooper, Van Morrison, the Mamas and the Papas, Frank Zappa, Janis Joplin, Otis Redding, Smokey Robinson, the Four Tops, and Jimi Hendrix.

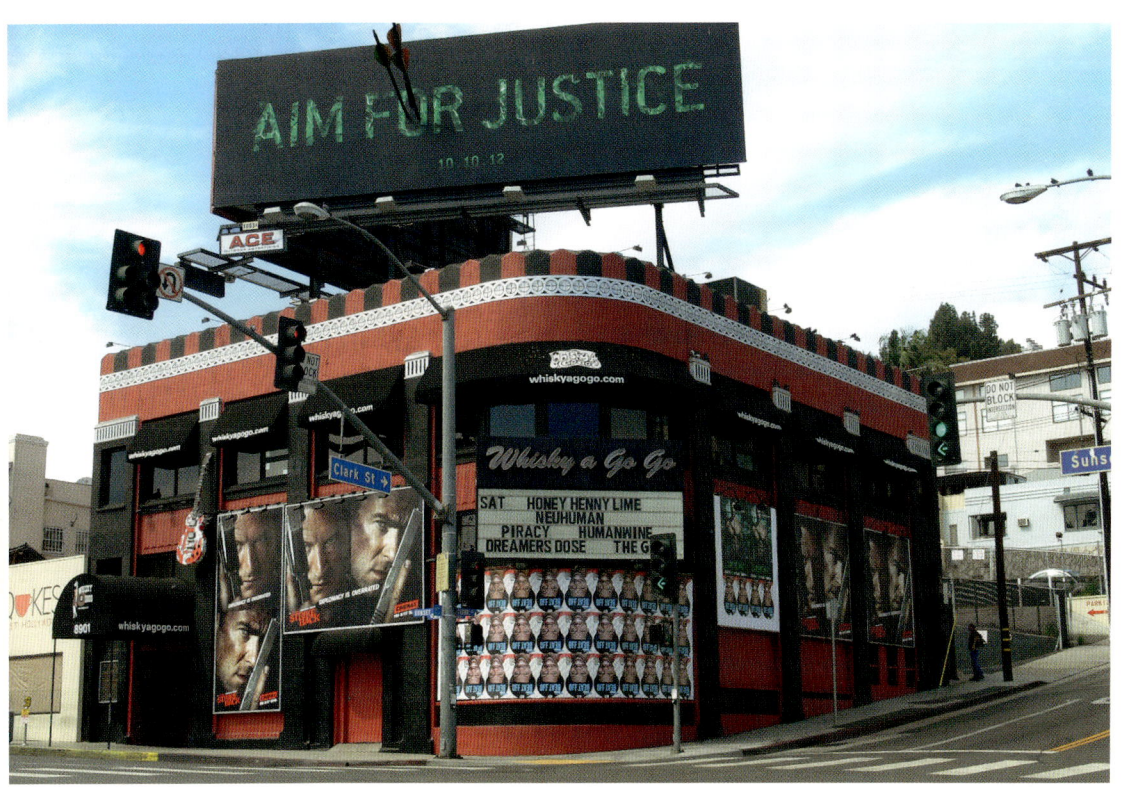

ABOVE: Through the decades, musicians from all spheres have found an audience here. The Whisky was instrumental in bringing punk and new wave to audiences on the West Coast. In turn, it hosted heavy metal and the grunge movement, with Mudhoney, Soundgarden, and Hole playing at the Whisky. Meanwhile, new Whisky a Go Go nightclubs opened up all over the world. Black Sabbath announced their reunion at the original Whisky in 2011. On January 16, 2014, Whisky a Go Go celebrated its fiftieth birthday on the Sunset Strip, commemorating five decades as a major part of Los Angeles nightlife.

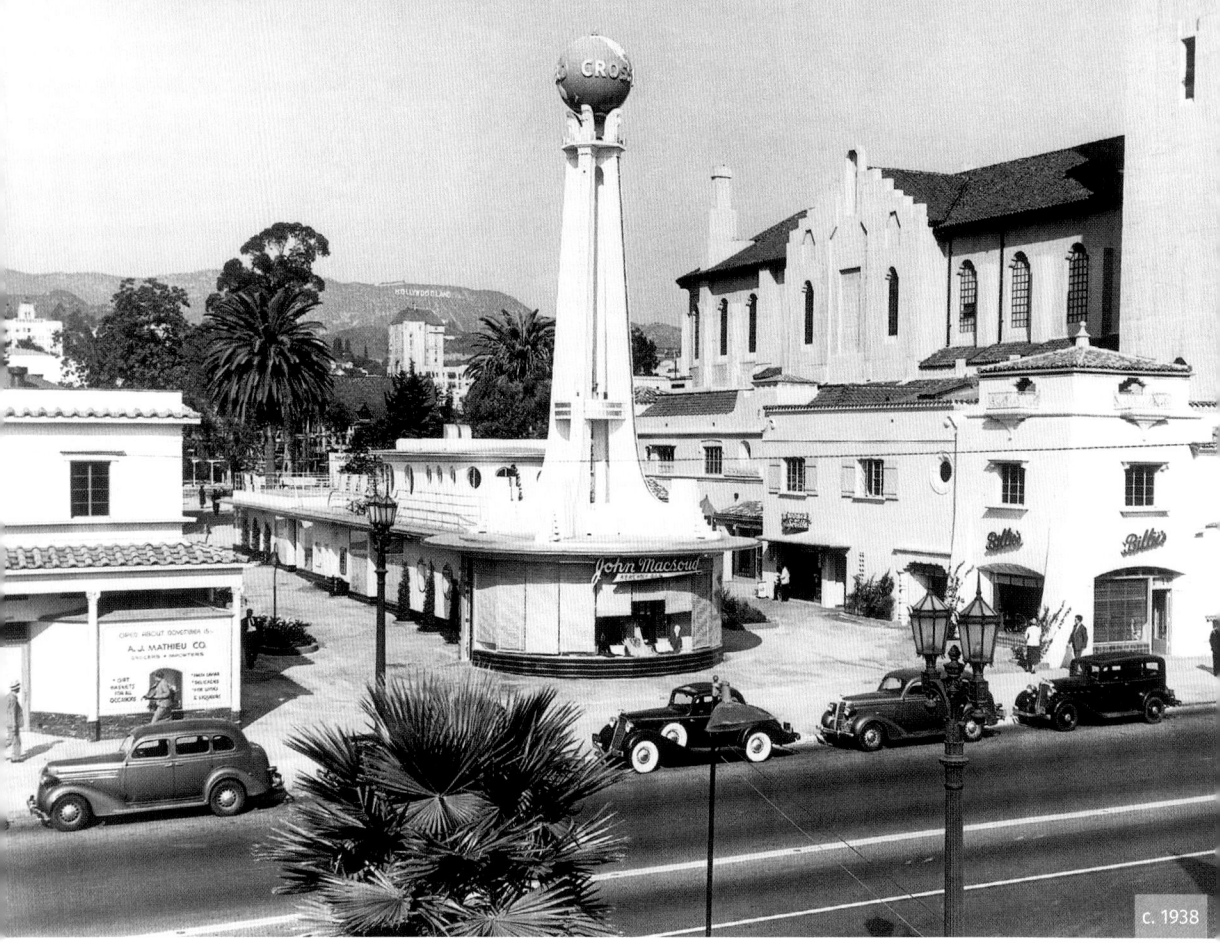

c. 1938

CROSSROADS OF THE WORLD

A striking development from the pen of Robert V. Derrah

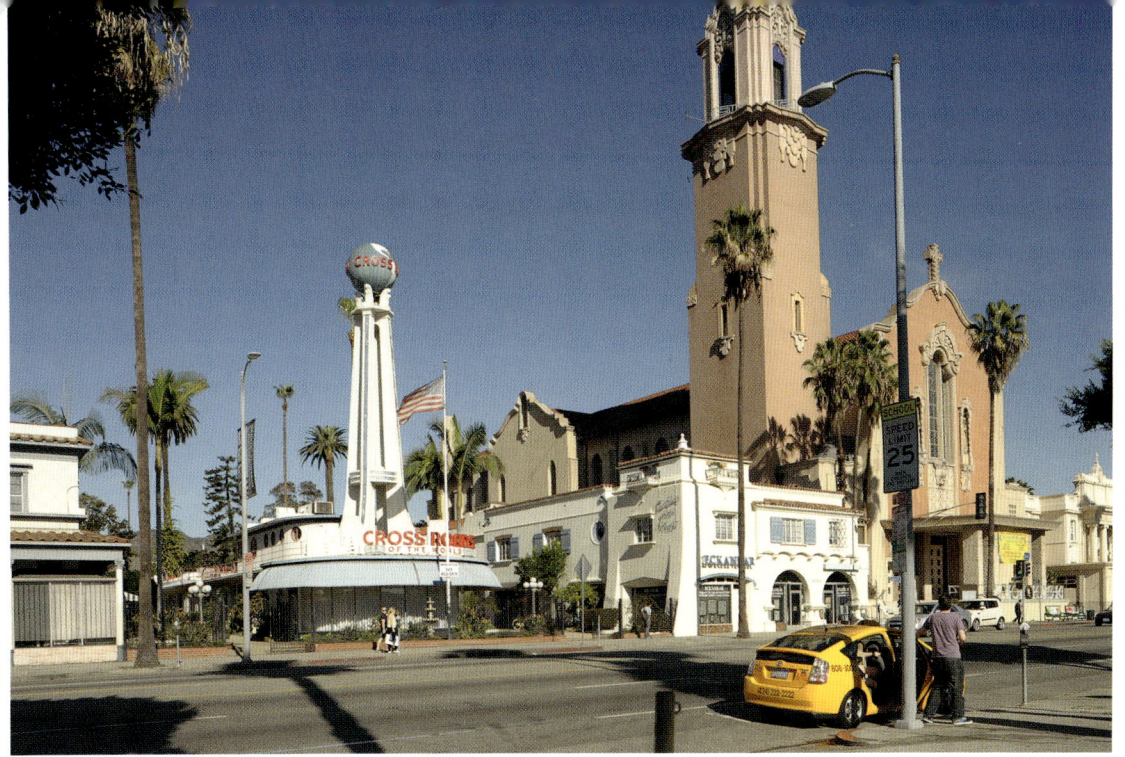

LEFT: Once called "L.A.'s first modern shopping mall," Crossroads of the World opened in 1936 on Sunset Boulevard, near Las Palmas. Boris Karloff, Cesar Romero, and Binnie Barnes were among the celebrities at the opening. The unique center building resembles a ship, complete with portholes and decks, as well as a thirty-foot tower topped by a revolving world globe. The bungalows surrounding this were a mixture of Italian, Spanish, French, and New England designs from architect Robert V. Derrah. This quaint pedestrian precinct with stylish boutiques was very popular from the 1930s through the 1960s.

ABOVE: The boutiques in Crossroads of the World have been replaced by small businesses and TV casting offices. Alfred Hitchcock and Tim Burton had offices here. The Church of the Blessed Sacrament is visible to the right. Plans are now afoot to develop this 1930s site. Facing opposition from local historic, preservation, and residents' organizations, the Harridge Development Group proposes that the eight-acre mixed-use plan would span from Sunset Boulevard on the south to Highland Avenue on the east. The cost of "Crossroads Hollywood" would be around $1 billion.

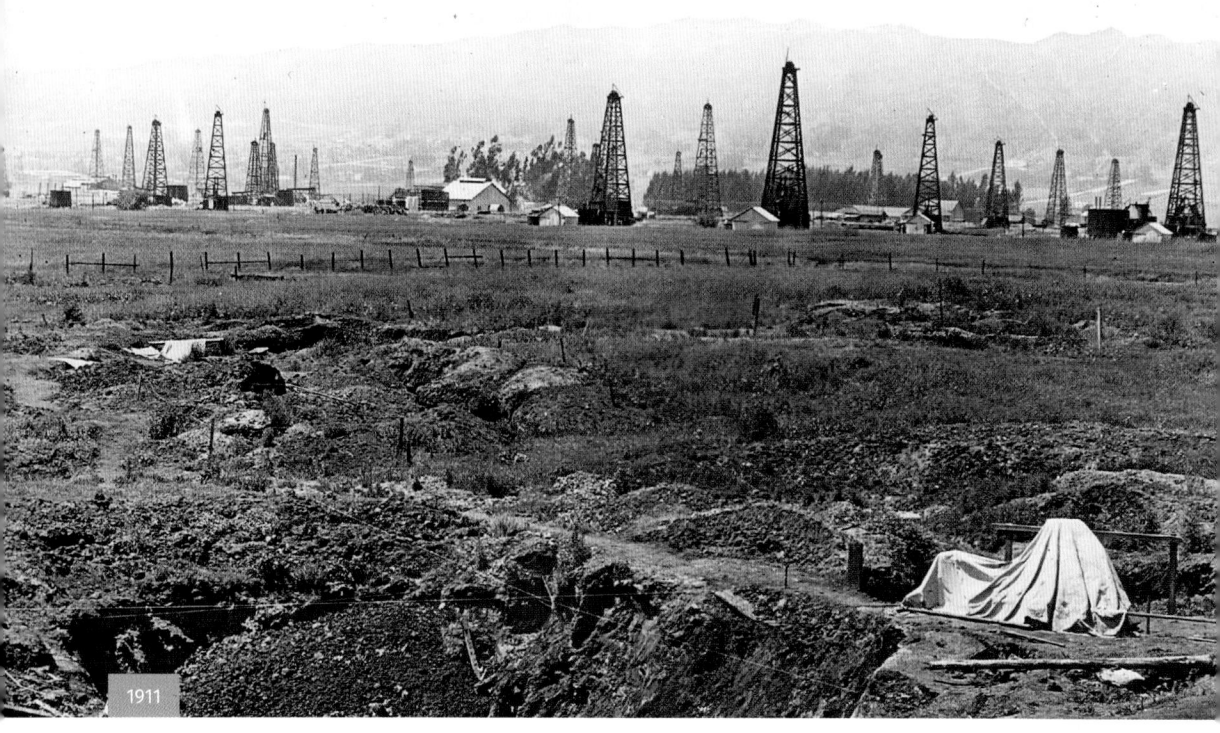

1911

LA BREA TAR PITS

Repository of a wide variety of pre–Ice Age flora and fauna

ABOVE: Fossil miners work at the La Brea Tar Pits in this 1911 photograph. At Rancho La Brea, tar (brea in Spanish) has been seeping up for thousands of years. Over the centuries, animals attracted by the surface water fell in, sank in the tar, and their bones were preserved. Humans found uses for the tar early on; Native Americans discovered the use of the tar for waterproofing purposes. Spanish explorers and settlers used the natural source of asphalt to caulk their ships and create waterproof roofing of early adobes. Around 1900, a worldwide fascination with dinosaurs, fossils, and anthropology emerged, but it wasn't until after World War II that new technologies made it possible for many more artifacts to be uncovered from the black depths of La Brea. A great number of large mammal skeletons were found, as well as the partial skeleton of a woman thought to date back 9,000 years.

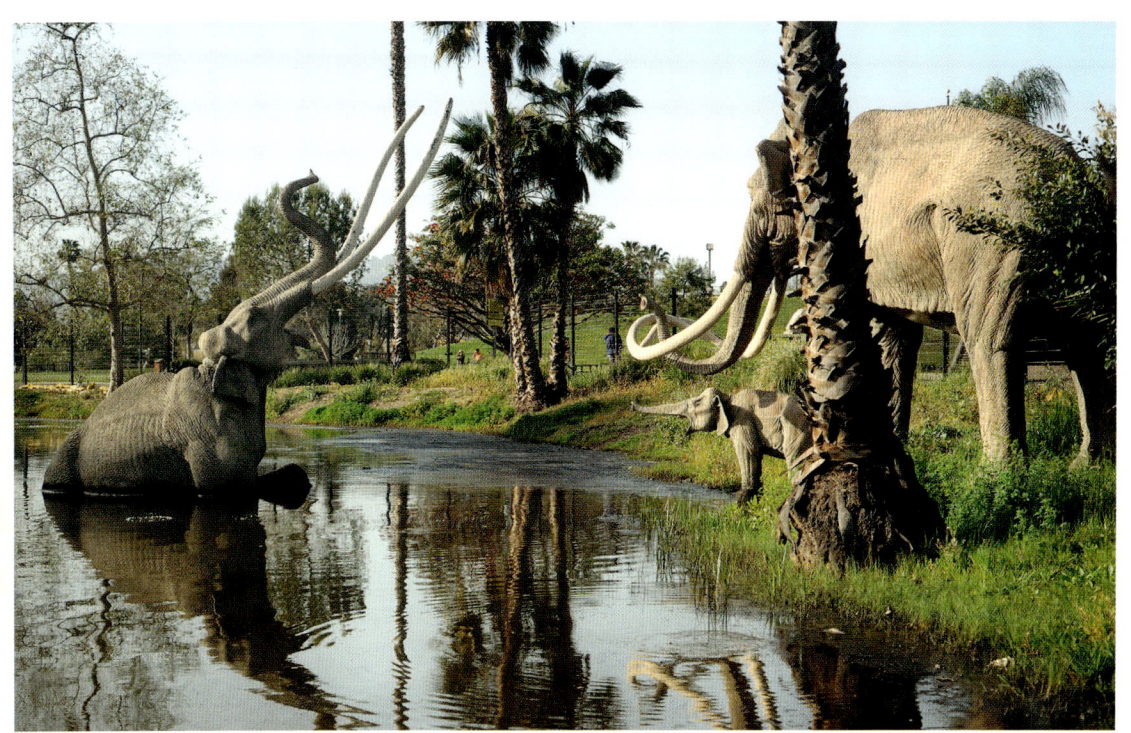

ABOVE: Fossils of the dire wolf, saber-toothed tiger, woolly mammoth, short-faced bear, and ground sloth have been found in the La Brea Tar Pits, in enough quantities to keep researchers busy well into the next century. The George C. Page Museum on the site is dedicated to researching the tar pits and displaying specimens from the animals that have been found there. Page built the museum from the fortune he made shipping oranges to places like his home state of Nebraska. The museum displays the largest and most diverse collection of extinct Ice Age plants and animals in the world. Through windows at the Page Museum Laboratory, visitors watch specialists clean and repair specimens. Outside, in Hancock Park, life-size replicas of several extinct mammals are featured. Once a year, visitors can view volunteers excavating the pits under the supervision of paleontologists.

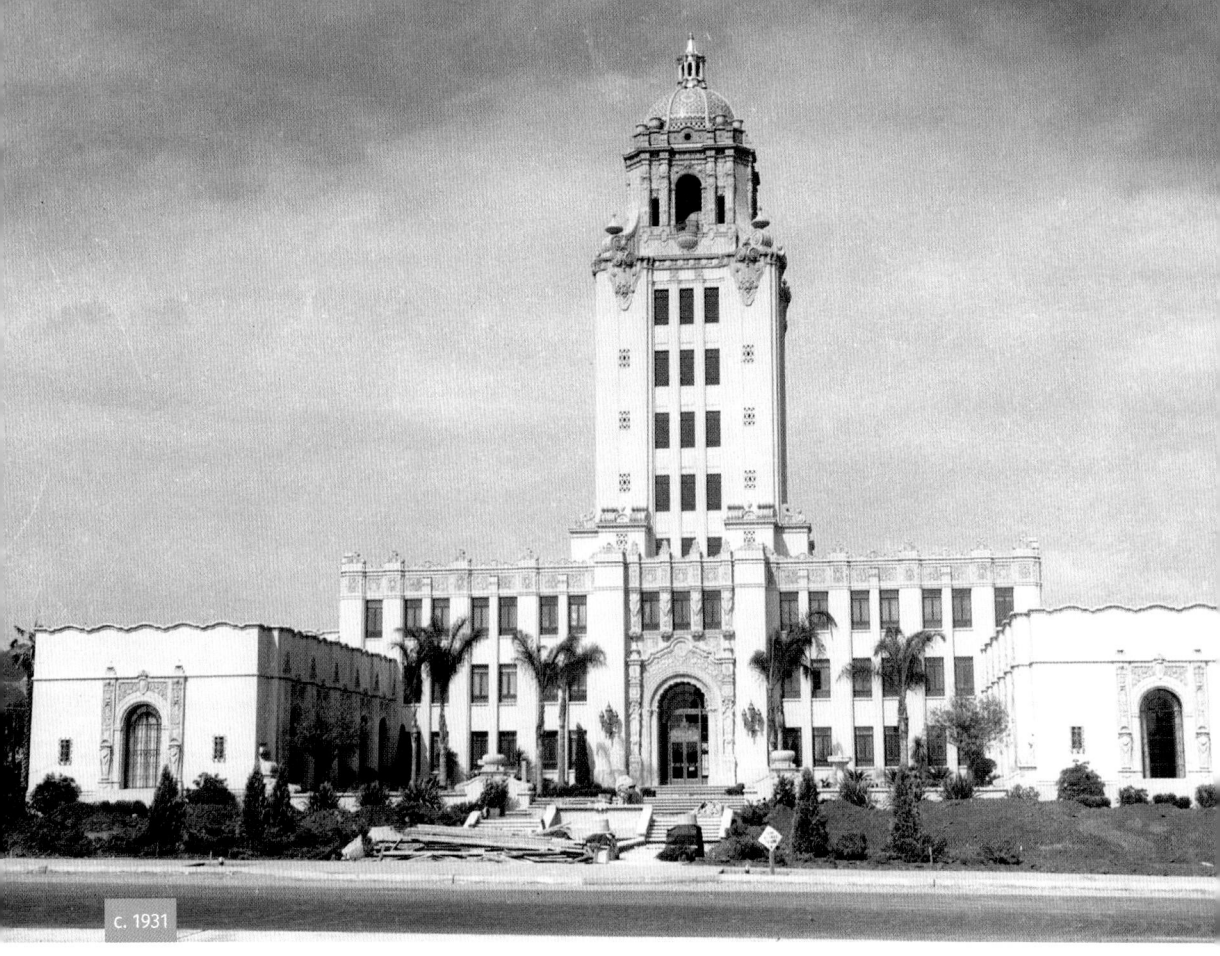

c. 1931

BEVERLY HILLS CITY HALL

The Beverly Hills City Hall is a complete contrast to that of Los Angeles

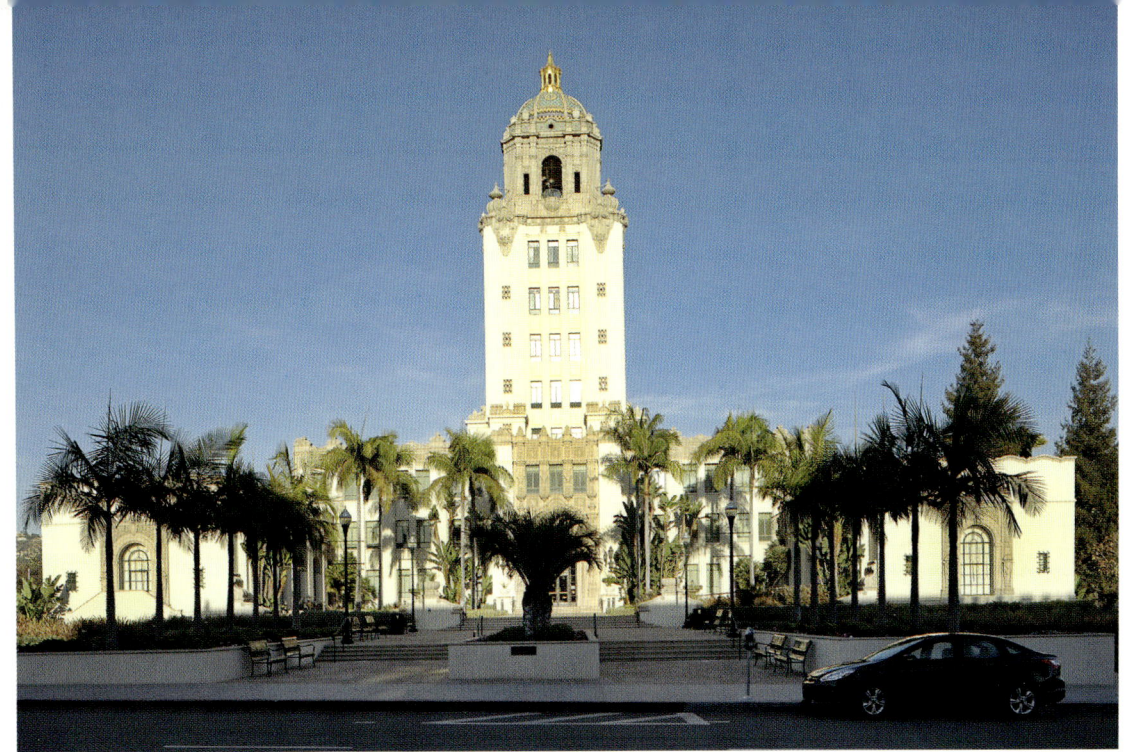

LEFT: In 1906 Burton Green formed the Rodeo Land and Water Company and planned a new, luxurious city, calling it Beverly Hills. It had previously been just a small train stop, called Morocco, on the route through the bean fields down to the ocean. The land was later sold for oil development. In 1919 Mary Pickford and Douglas Fairbanks built their famous home, Pickfair, and launched the migration of motion-picture people to the area. The Beverly Hills City Hall, as seen here, was built in 1931 in a bean field. Designed by architect William Gage in the Spanish Renaissance style, the building opened in 1932.

ABOVE: Carefully planned, the city has strict zoning laws. While stars of Hollywood's golden age—such as Elizabeth Taylor, Gene Kelly, Jimmy Stewart, Kirk Douglas, and George Burns—used to live in Beverly Hills, many of today's residents are the foreign born wealthy. The Beverly Hills Civic Center, designed by Charles Moore in 1988, links the new library and the police and fire departments with the historic Spanish-style city hall at 455 North Rexford Drive. The governors of this city hall coordinated the many commemorative activities for the 2014 yearlong City of Beverly Hills centennial.

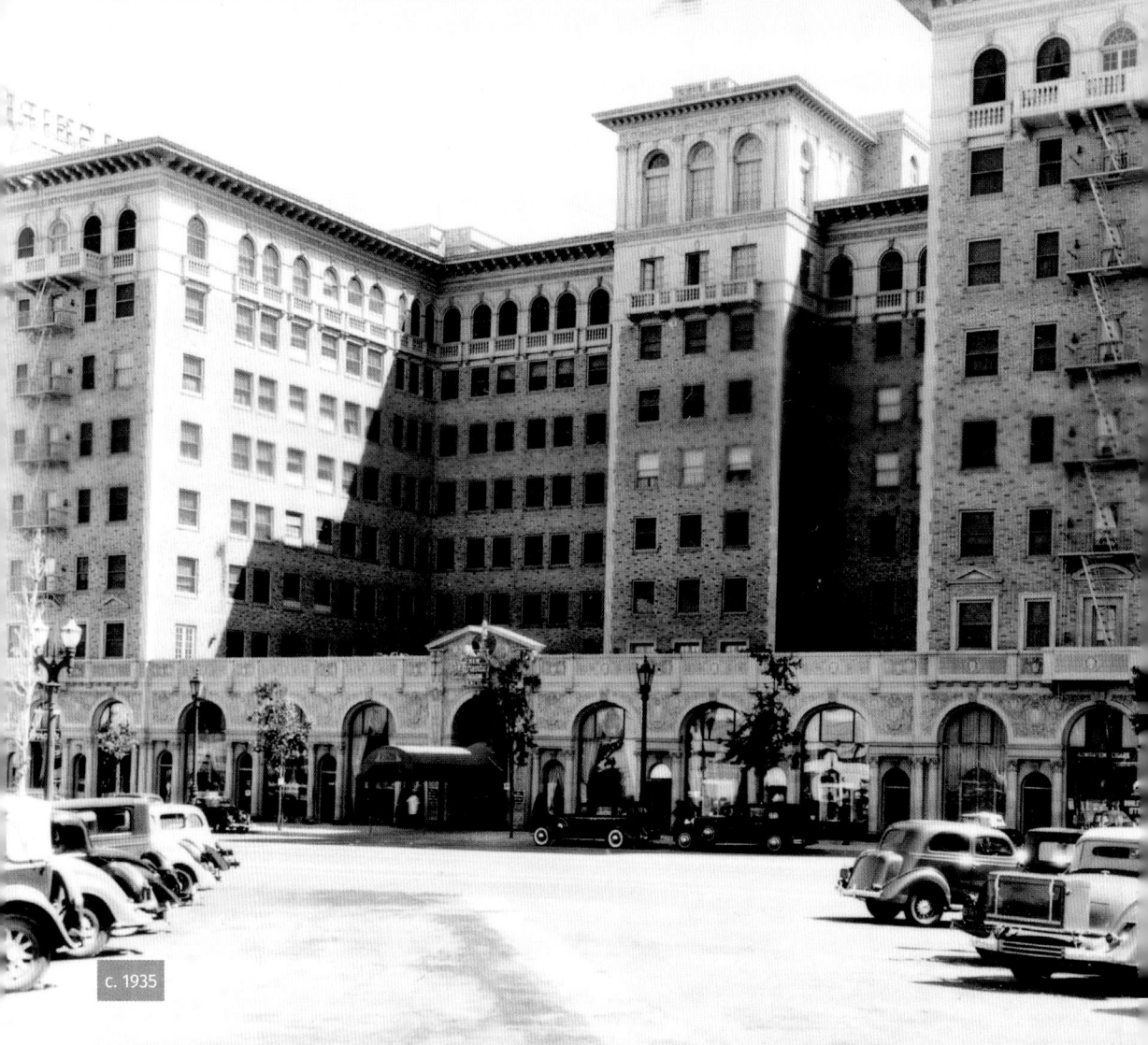

c. 1935

BEVERLY WILSHIRE HOTEL

The Beverly Hills Speedway made way for this grand hotel

LEFT: In the 1920s, the Beverly Hills Speedway was always packed with spectators, including celebrities like Wallace Beery, Charlie Chaplin, and Tom Mix. The autodrome closed in 1924 when some of the land (between Wilshire Boulevard and Pico, from Beverly Drive to Lasky) was needed to create the swank Beverly Wilshire Hotel. Built in 1927 by the Courtright family, the elegant hotel was an immediate success. Over the years, Dashiell Hammett wrote *The Thin Man* at the Wilshire, Cary Grant and Elvis Presley were residents, and Steve McQueen kept his motorcycles on site.

BELOW: The hotel is where Rodeo Drive now meets Wilshire Boulevard. John Lennon stayed here, and Warren Beatty and Elvis Presley both rented the penthouse. Julia Roberts and Richard Gere stayed here in *Pretty Woman*—as did Eddie Murphy in *Beverly Hills Cop.* Hernando Courtright sold the hotel in 1985, when it became the Regent Beverly Wilshire Hotel. In 2006 the hotel became the Beverly Wilshire, a Four Seasons hotel. It was listed on the National Register of Historic Places in 1987.

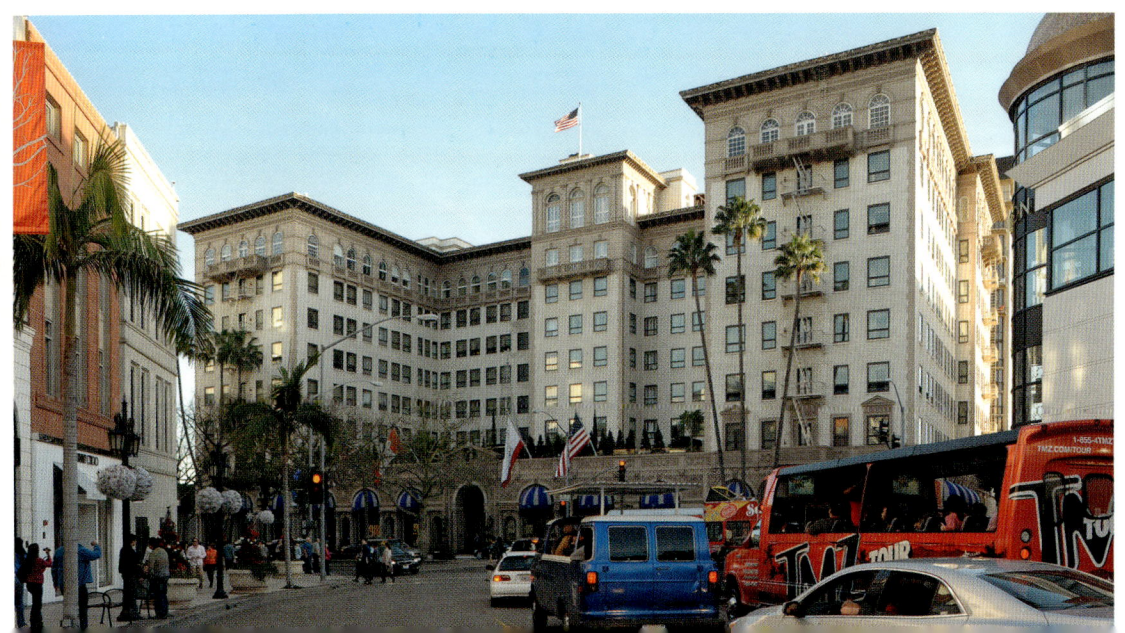

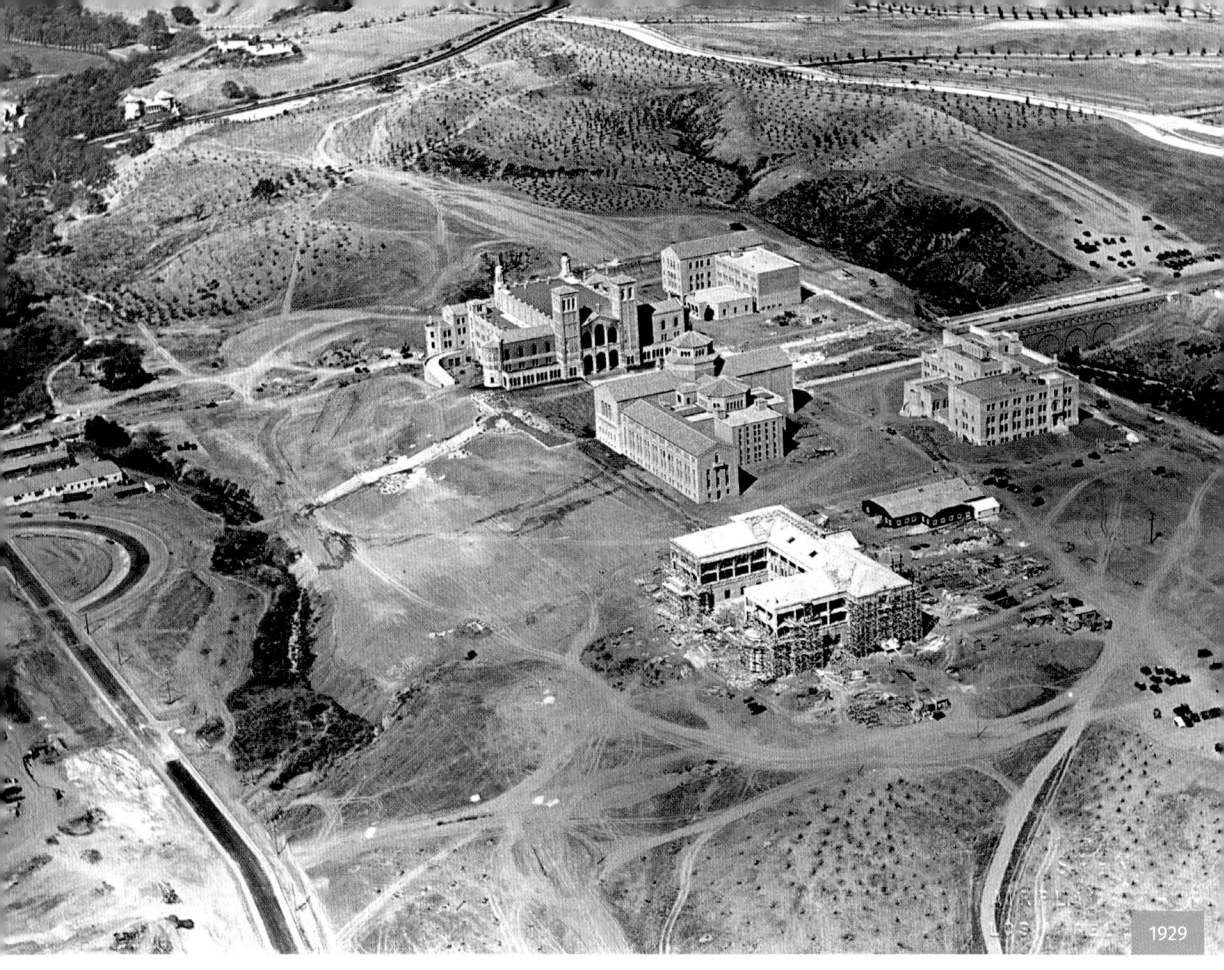

1929

UCLA

The University of California, Los Angeles, has never stopped growing

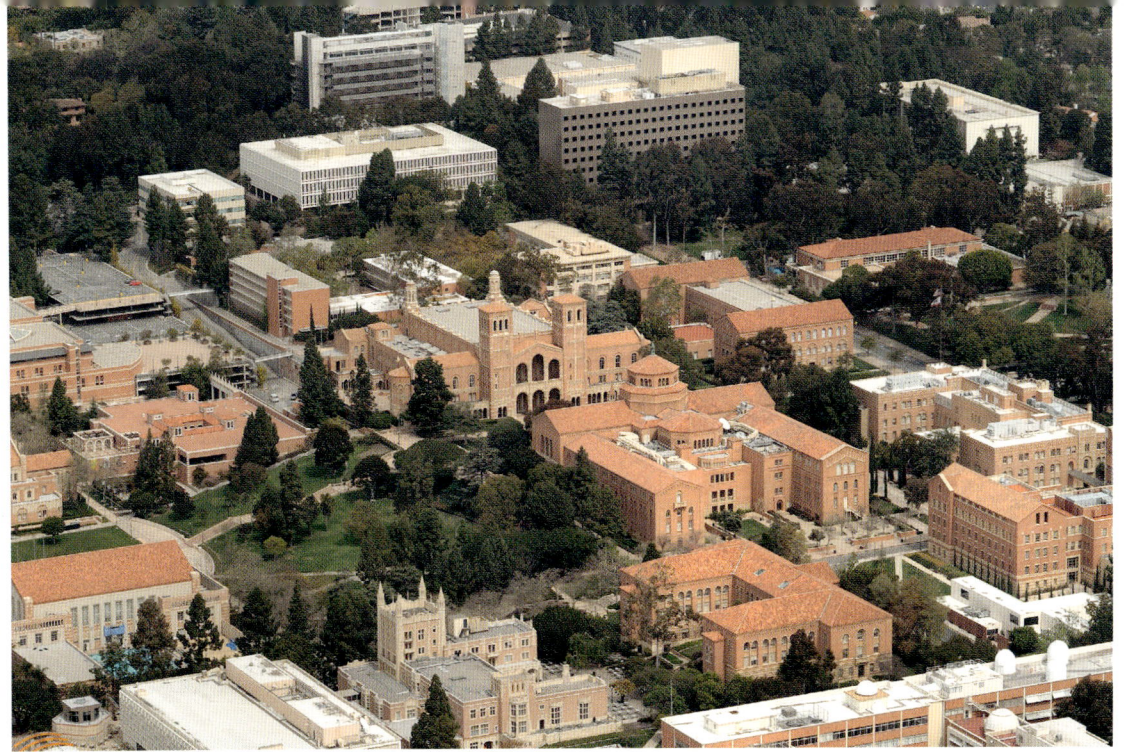

LEFT: The University of California, Los Angeles (UCLA), seen here in 1929, is a public university founded in 1919. The school grew so fast that just a decade after its founding, it needed a larger campus. The new campus was undergoing construction in 1929, the year of this photograph. Architects designed all five campus buildings in the Romanesque Revival style. The first class to graduate at the new Westwood campus had 5,500 students. The first master's degrees were awarded in 1933, and the first doctorate in 1936. Royce Hall, with its pair of steeples, is seen at left center of the main photo; the domed Powell Library sits across from it.

ABOVE: One nickname for UCLA is "Under Construction Like Always." The student population continues to grow, and construction and renovation projects are nearly continuous. Royce Hall and the Powell Library still anchor the heart of the campus. With just four buildings at its onset, the campus now has over 163 buildings to serve its student body. Campus amenities include sculpture gardens, fountains, museums, and a mile from campus in Bel Air, a Japanese garden.

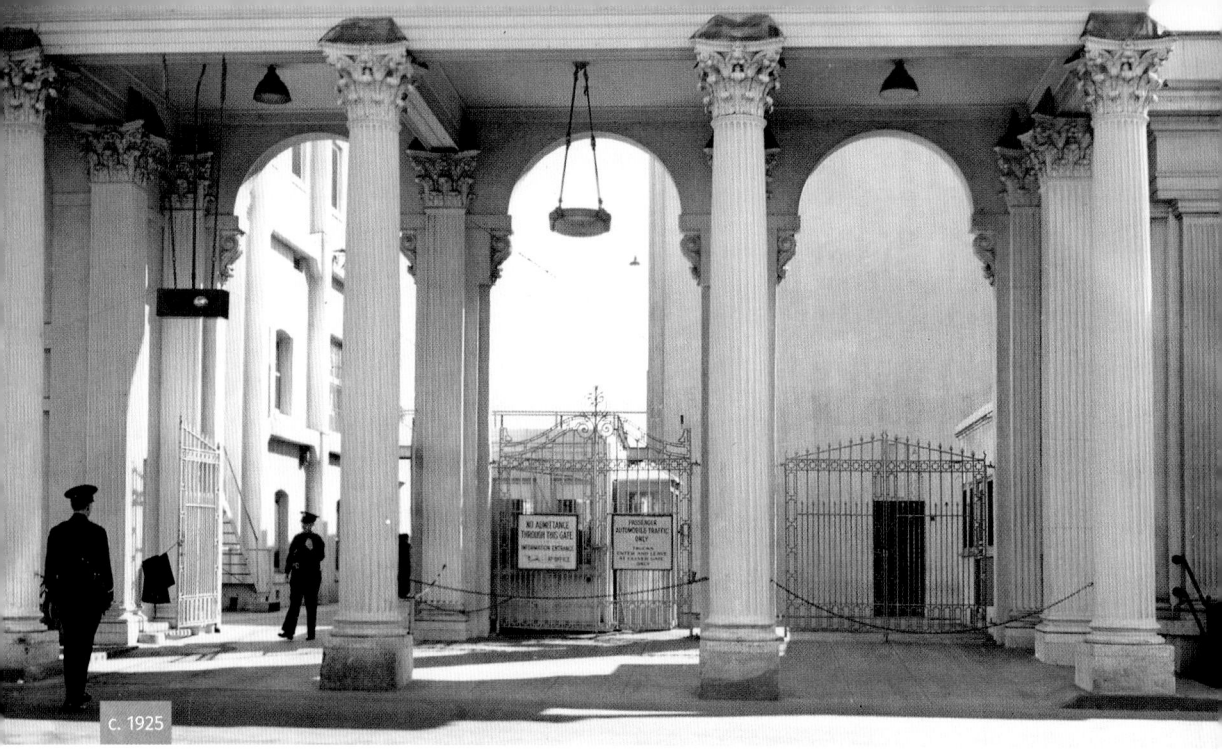

c. 1925

MGM-SONY STUDIOS

"Do it right, do it big, give it class"

ABOVE: Founded in 1924 under Louis B. Mayer's guidance, Metro-Goldwyn-Mayer Studios was best known for musicals such as *The Wizard of Oz, Singin' in the Rain*, and the Fred Astaire–Ginger Rogers films. The original main gate was on Washington Boulevard in Culver City. MGM Studios covered more than 180 acres of land and was divided into six working studio complexes, known as "lots." At the front of the studios, Lot One was the (Irving) Thalberg Building, housing the production, casting, and other administration offices. Also on this lot were makeup and hairdressing, special effects, film labs, publicity, a commissary, and a barbershop. MGM had twenty-eight soundstages. Epics such as *Mutiny on the Bounty* and *Ben Hur* were filmed on the vast backlots.

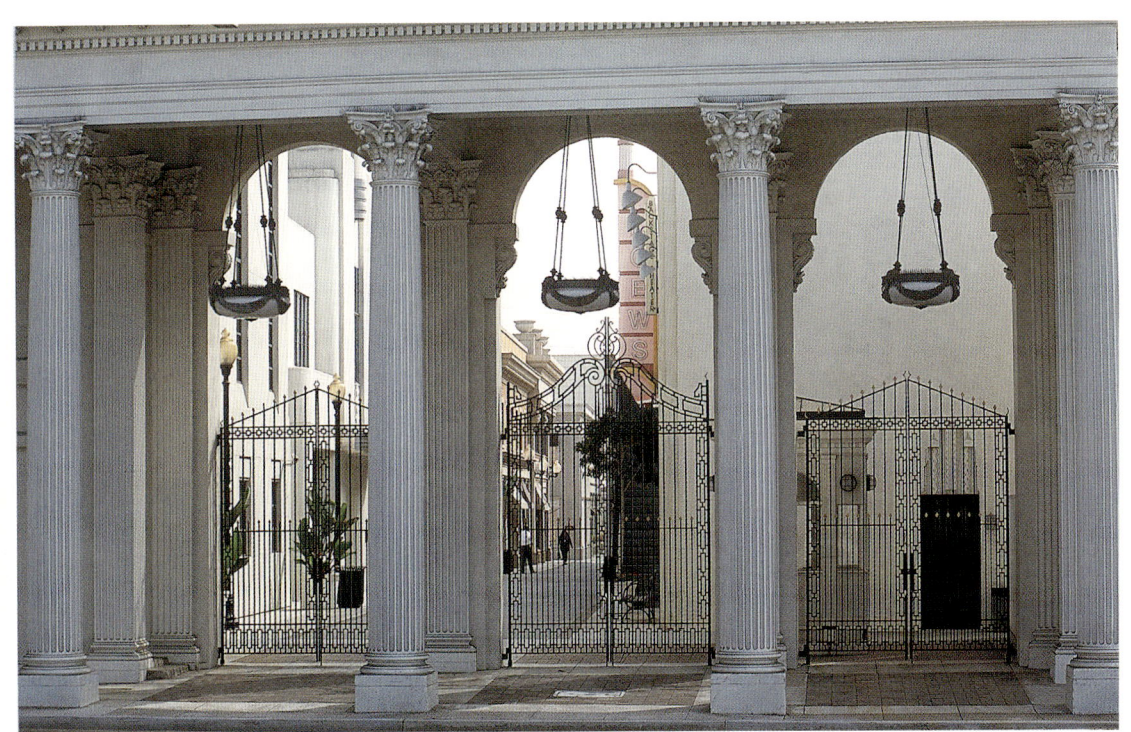

ABOVE: Like many studios that caught a financial chill from the postwar preference for television, MGM started to lose money and their extensive production facilities—which had once been their major asset—now became an unsustainable overhead. The old company motto of "Do it right, do it big, give it class" had to be set aside. The company began selling off backlots to be converted into real-estate tracts. MGM merged with United Artists in 1980 and then sold their famous studios to Lorimar Television. In 1990 Sony Entertainment took over what remained of the old MGM lot. Once the owners of the largest, most glamorous studio, MGM is now run from offices in Beverly Hills. Sony spent $100 million renovating the former MGM lot, which now has one of the best postproduction facilities. The film and television studio complex is home to long-running game shows *Jeopardy!* and *Wheel of Fortune*.

THELMA TODD'S CAFÉ

Thelma Todd was a femme fatale who lived up to her billing

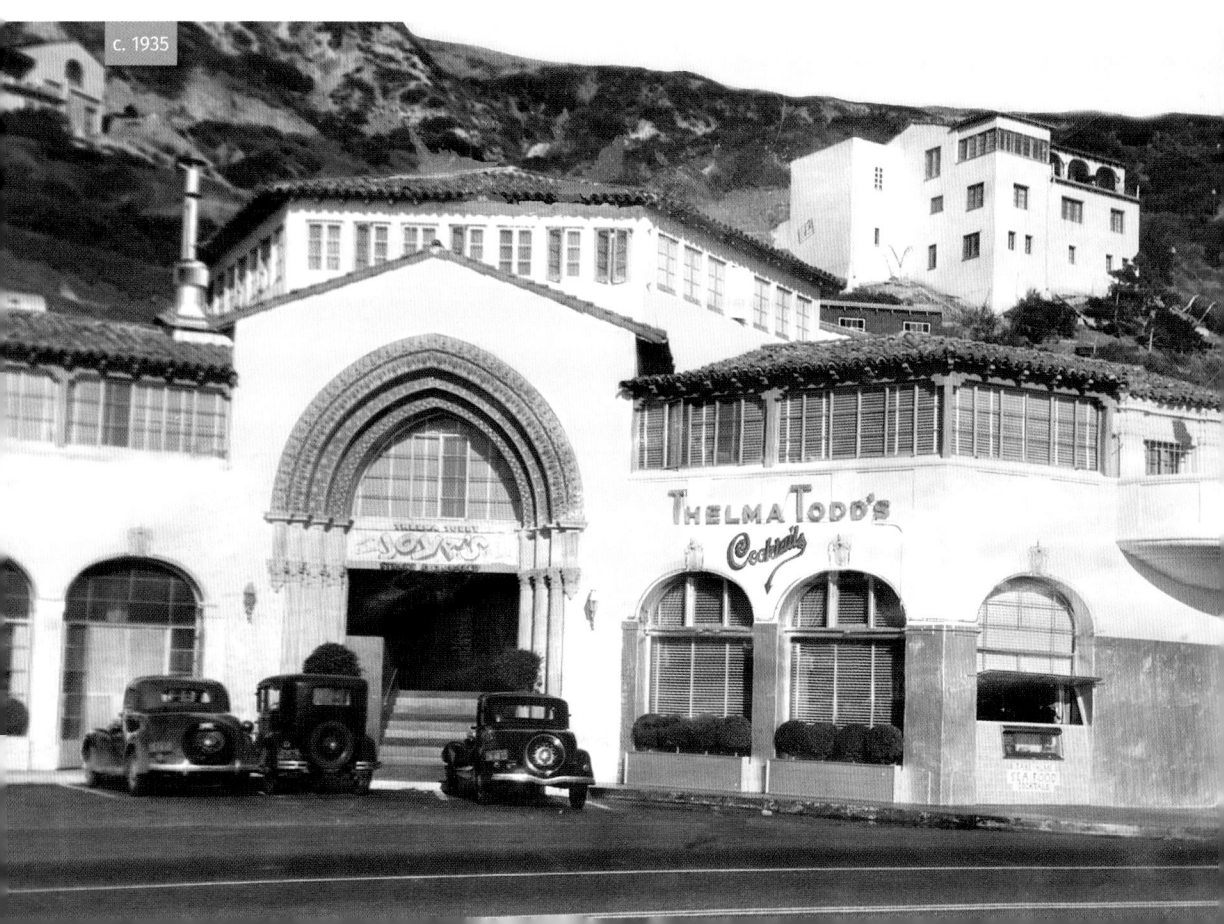

c. 1935

LEFT: Thelma Todd was an actress in the Jean Harlow mold. In the 1930s she appeared in several Marx Brothers comedies, including *Horse Feathers* and *Monkey Business*. She also ran Thelma Todd's Café, which overlooked the ocean at 17575 Pacific Coast Highway between Malibu and Pacific Palisades. In 1935 she was found dead in her car in the garage of former silent movie star Jewel Carmen. The police investigation ruled her death an "accidental suicide" from carbon monoxide poisoning, but the puzzling aspect was that she had a bloodied lip. There were no other marks of a violent struggle, but Todd did not leave a suicide note.

BELOW: A cover-up was suspected, but the mystery was never solved. The Chez Roland Beach Club took over through 1950. After years of neglect, the building was bought by Paulist Productions. Founded by Father Elwood Kaiser in 1968 it is dedicated to producing "uplifting entertainment that unifies the human family." Mostly shown on the TNT and Hallmark channels, Paulist produced the Insight series and has been working on the true story of Home Boy Industries, a gang recovery program. Employees in the production offices claim to have seen Thelma Todd's ghost walking down the stairs.

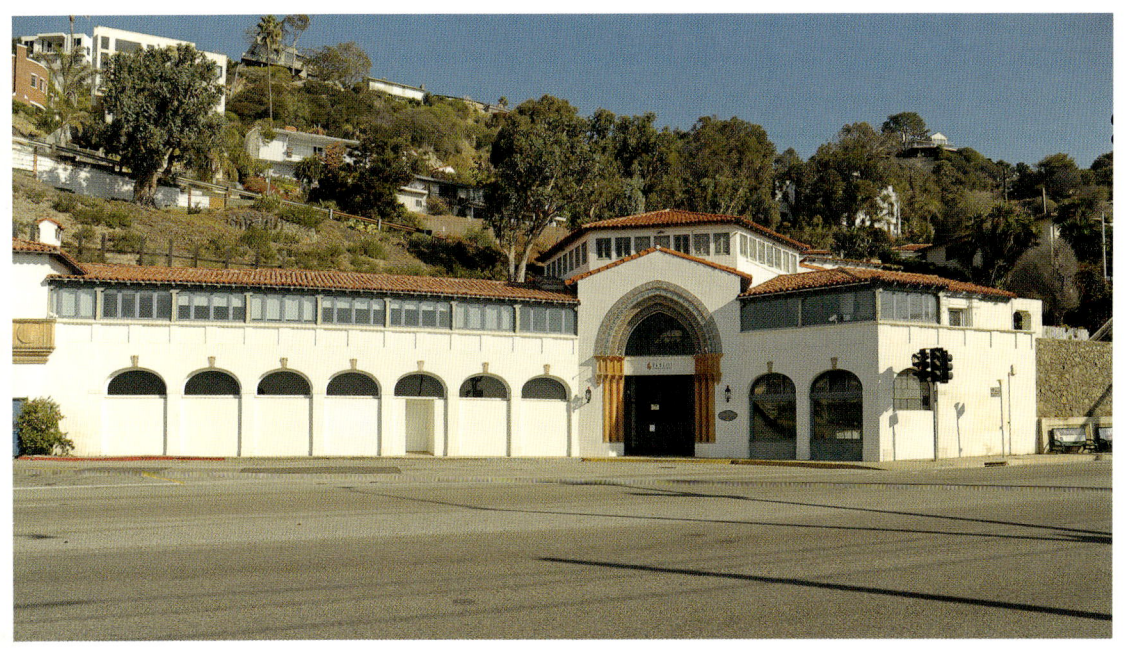

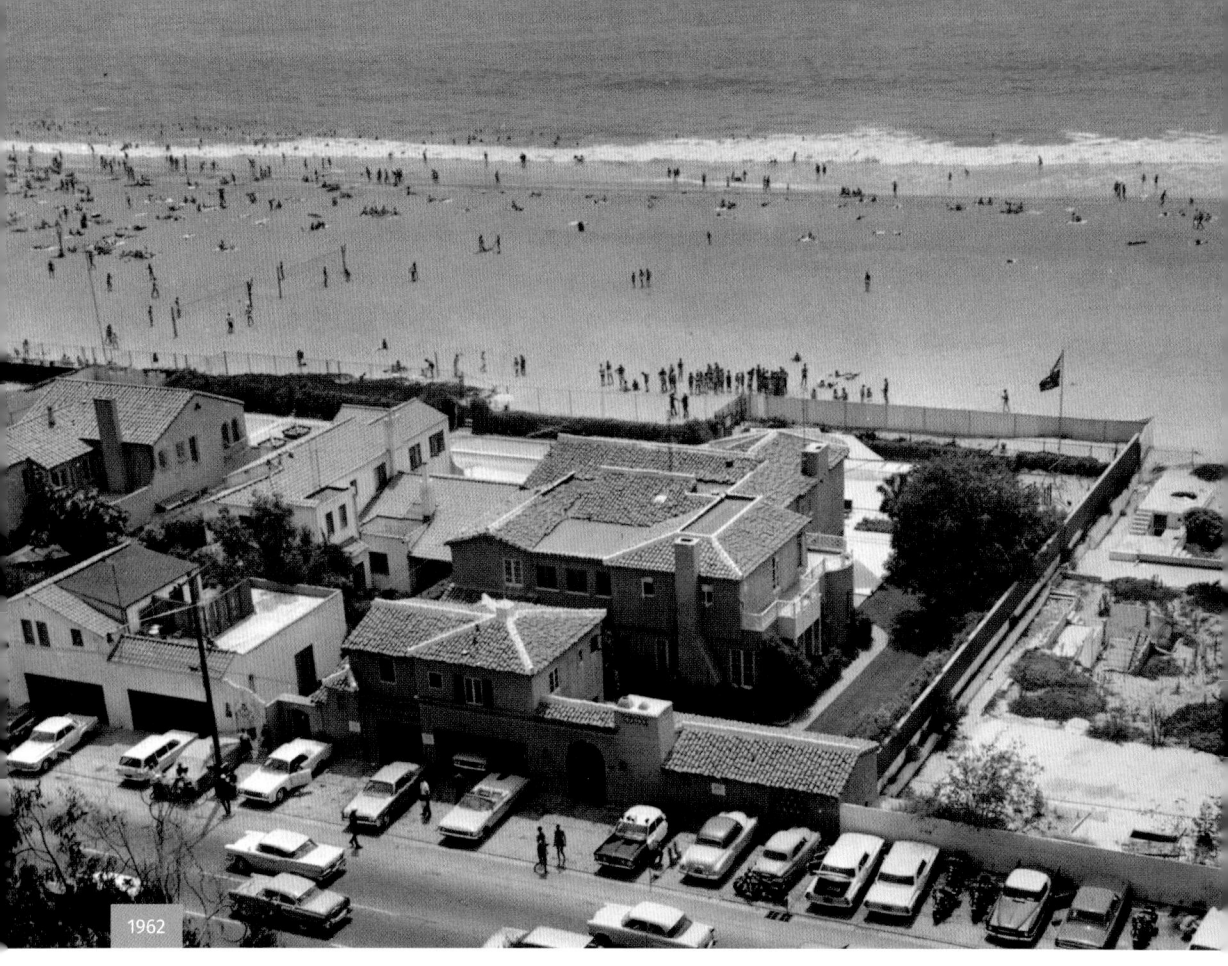

1962

LOUIS B. MAYER HOUSE

John F. Kennedy would often drop by to see his sister Pat Lawford

86

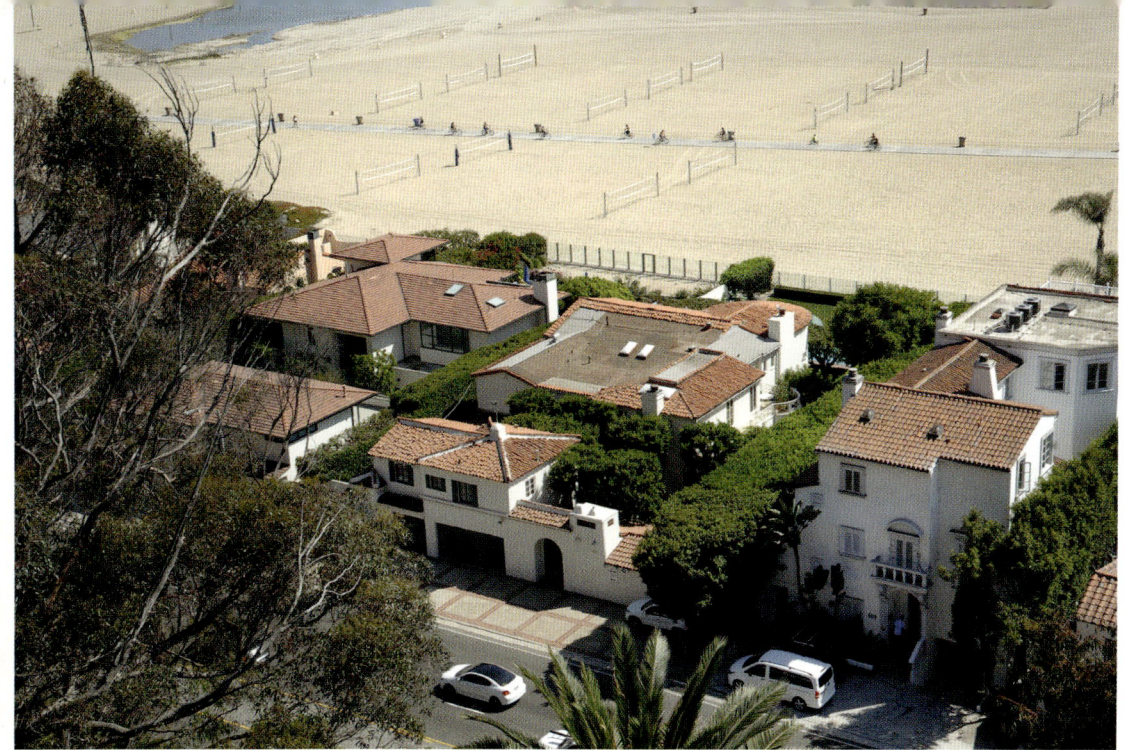

LEFT: The Palisades Beach Road in Santa Monica was home to many movie stars in the 1920s and 30s. Douglas Fairbanks, Harold Lloyd, Mae West, Norma Shearer and Samuel Goldwyn were all neighbors. In 1926 MGM co-founder, Louis B. Mayer, bought the oceanfront property at 625, known as Rancho San Vicente. The Spanish-style house was built in just six weeks and cost $26,000. The house featured wooden beams, wrought-iron balconies, an oceanfront swimming pool and a gatekeeper's apartment. There was a private projection room where *Gone With The Wind* was first screened.

ABOVE: English-born actor Peter Lawford bought the house in 1956 for $95,000. Lawford co-starred in *Easter Parade* with Judy Garland and was part of the famous "Rat Pack" that included Frank Sinatra, Dean Martin, and Sammy Davis Jr. They visited the house often. Lawford's wife, Pat Kennedy, was the sister of President John F. Kennedy. John and his brother Robert were frequent guests, as were many starlets—including Marilyn Monroe. The house was later rented out as "party central" during the late 1960s and 70s. In 1974 John Lennon, Ringo Starr, and Paul McCartney spent time there.

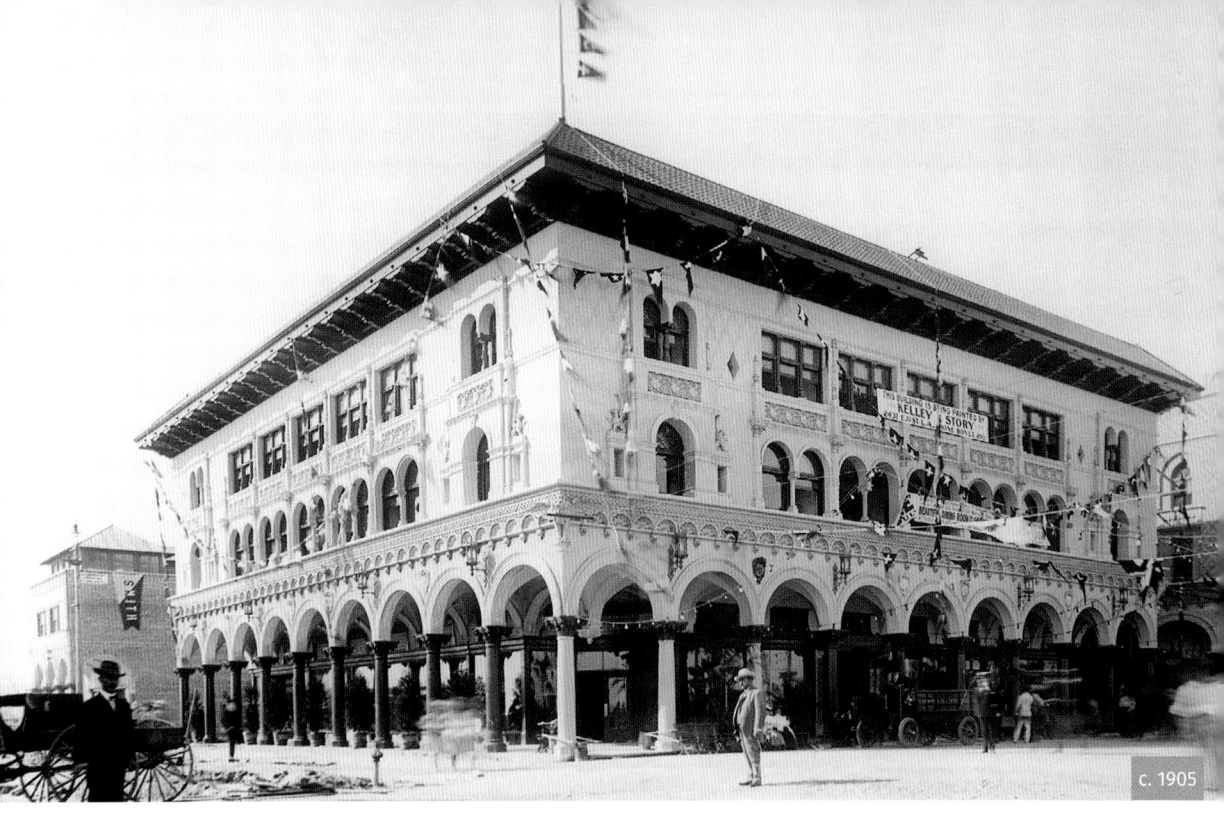

c. 1905

ST. MARK'S HOTEL

Developer Abbot Kinney wanted to capitalize on the cachet of Venice

ABOVE: In 1904 entrepreneur Abbot Kinney established a beachfront theme park called Venice of America. Architect Norman E. March emulated Venice, Italy, when designing this new area, which drew crowds to the ocean. On July 4, 1905, Kinney invited thousands of potential buyers to Venice's grand opening. The centerpiece was the elegant, columned St. Mark's Hotel. Catering to the rich and famous, St. Mark's welcomed stars such as Charlie Chaplin, Sarah Bernhardt, Theda Bara, and Douglas Fairbanks, who also enjoyed the Venice Casino and Dance Pavilion.

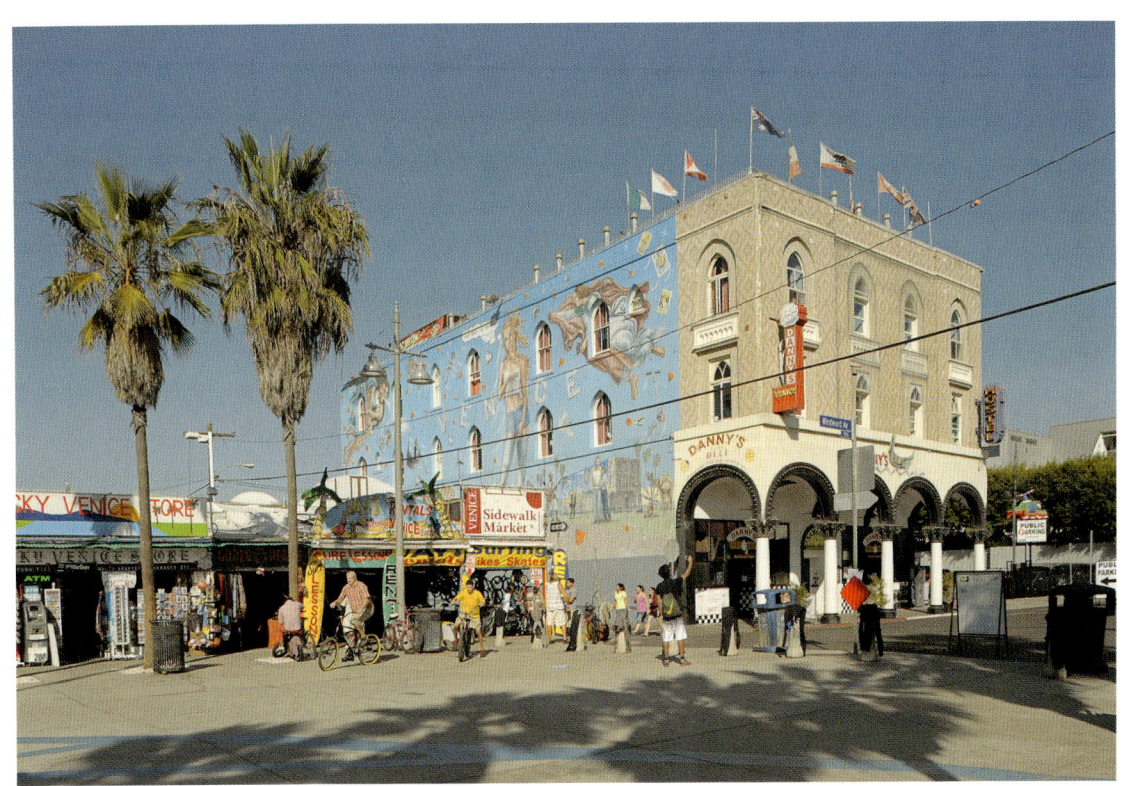

ABOVE: The Depression of the 1930s took its toll on Venice, and eventually the St. Mark's Hotel was abandoned. By the 1970s, many of the beautiful Italianate buildings had crumbled or were demolished, and the arched windows were filled in or modernized. The original Hotel St. Mark has disappeared, but the building seen here is one of the few reminders of Windward Avenue's rich architectural past. Since the late 1990s, architects and New Agers have rediscovered this historical resort and have been restoring the area. The old building took the name St. Mark's for a while, but is now a popular eatery called Danny's.

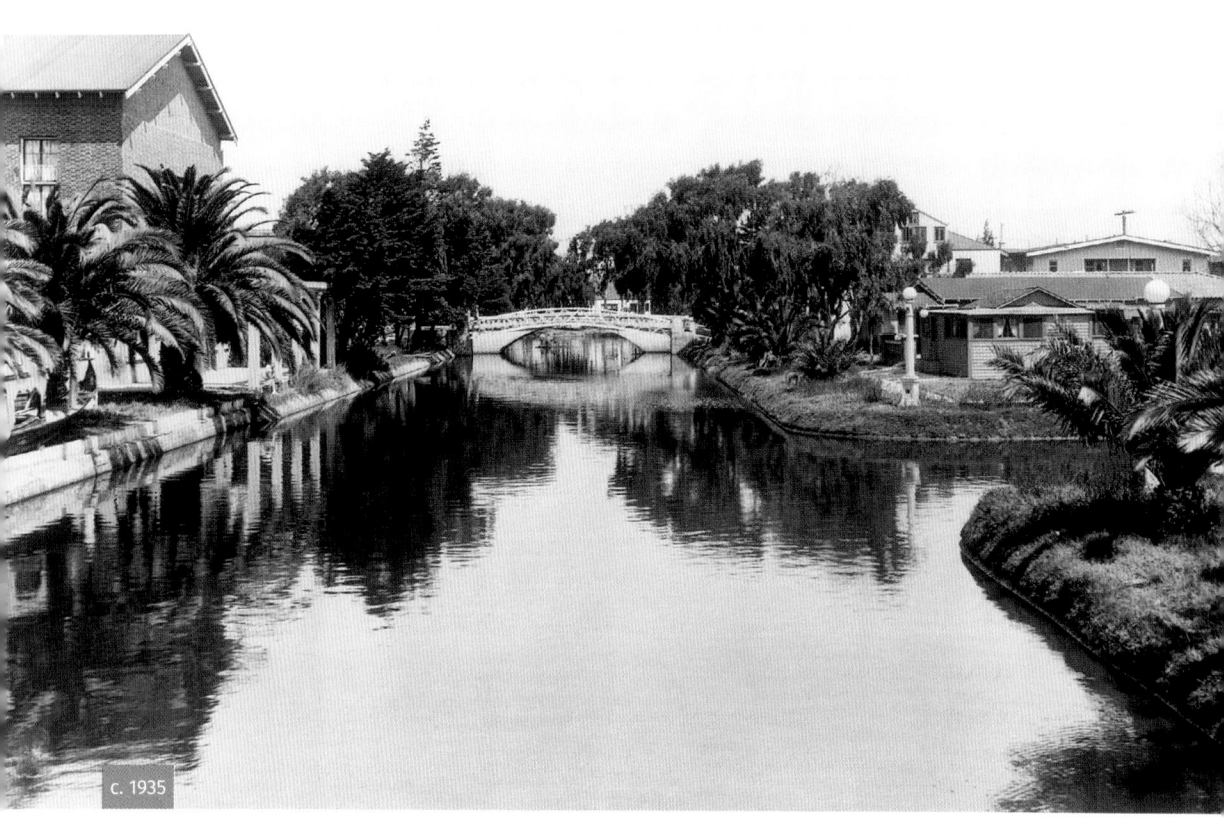

c. 1935

VENICE CANAL
A problem with drainage and eroding concrete spoiled Kinney's grand canal vision

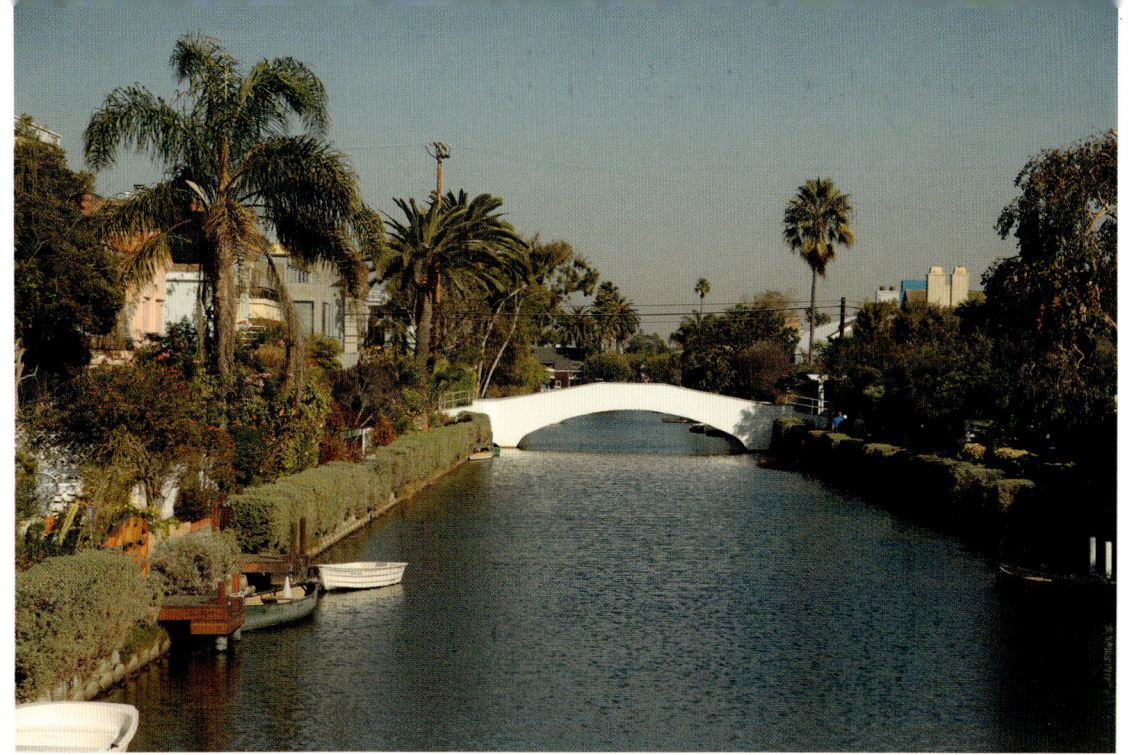

LEFT: In 1904, when Abbot Kinney was building Venice, he envisioned a fleet of Venetian gondoliers poling their way through interconnecting canals. Sixteen miles of canals were dug from salt marshes, bungalows were built alongside them, and people took to their boats and enjoyed water carnivals. Unfortunately, the canals were cheaply constructed with unreinforced concrete and soon the banks began to erode. Water started to undermine the sidewalks and the canals were steadily filled with pollution, sediment, and rubble. In 1942 the majority were withdrawn from public use and paved over.

ABOVE: Artists and hippies loved living here, and Jim Morrison of the Doors called the area home during the 1960s. The Grand Canal, at Windward and Main, where all the waterways connected, has long been paved over. In the 1980s, as real-estate prices soared, the bohemian canal-dwellers were replaced by the wealthy. In 1994 the city finally refurbished the six remaining canals. Still a magnet for artists and filmmakers, the canals—with a myriad of quaint bridges—run through a picturesque and tranquil neighborhood.

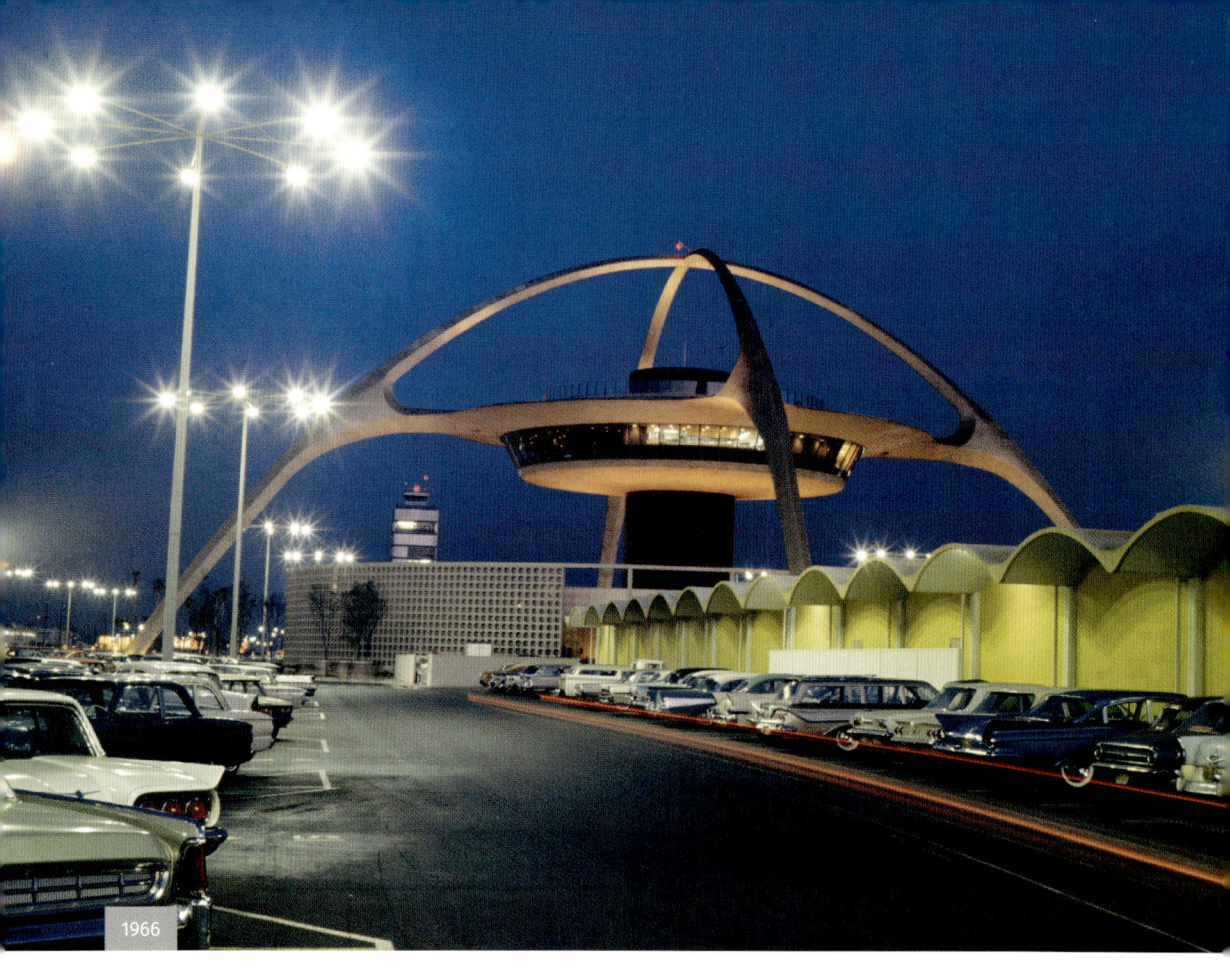

1966

THE THEME BUILDING, LAX

A space-age building towering over the world's fifth-busiest airport

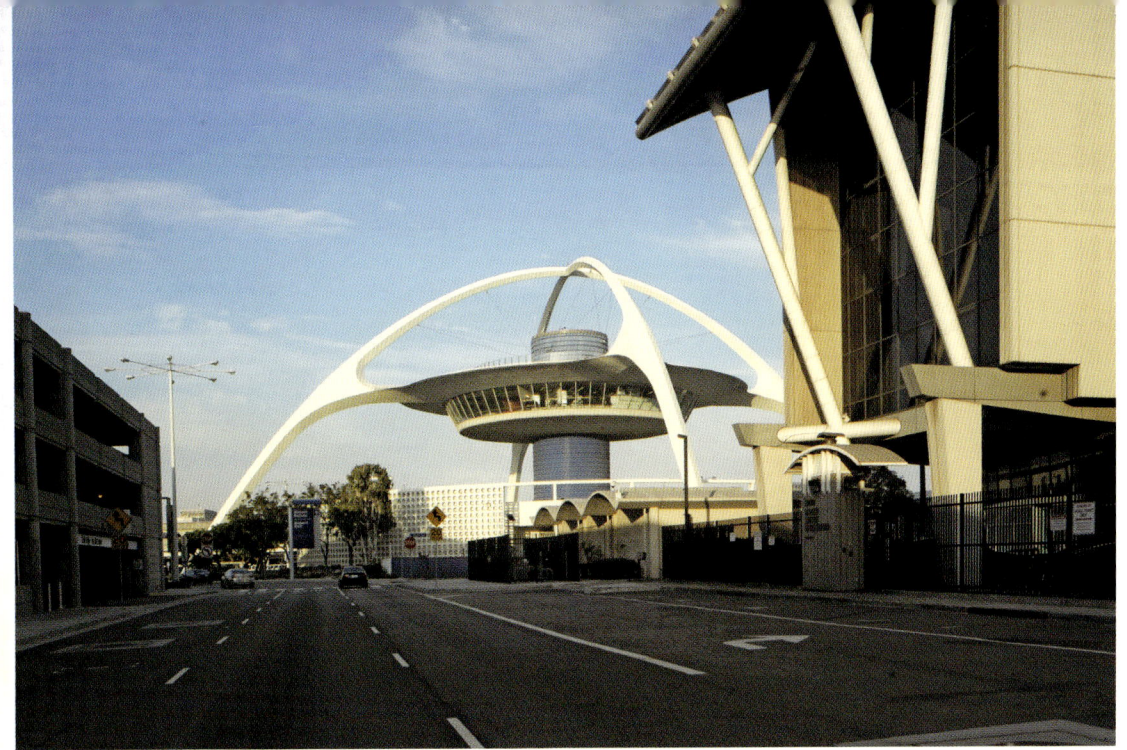

LEFT: Los Angeles's main airport, LAX, is built on an area called Mines Field near Inglewood. Since 1928 it was the Los Angeles Municipal Airport, serving the army, navy, air force and small commercial planes. By the late 1950s the airport had been developed into the Los Angeles International Airport, known as LAX. In 1961 the iconic space-age Theme Building opened at a cost of $50 million. The flying-saucer shaped design was created by William Pereira, Charles Luckman, Paul Williams, and Welton Becket. In the beginning, the restaurant on the top rotated slowly, providing a unique dining experience, but it was later made stationary.

ABOVE: The structure was designated a Los Angles Historic-Cultural Monument in 1993. The Walt Disney Imagineering team then designed a $4 million renovation and the new Encounter Restaurant opened in 1997. In 2007 a $14.3 million seismic upgrade and retrofit was started after a half-ton chunk of stucco fell onto the restaurant roof. New engineering was used for the arch system and a unique 600-ton, tuned mass damper was installed in the roof to absorb any earthquake motion. A people-mover system will link the building with the main arteries of the airport as part of the new $14 Billion L.A.X. renovation due to complete in 2023.

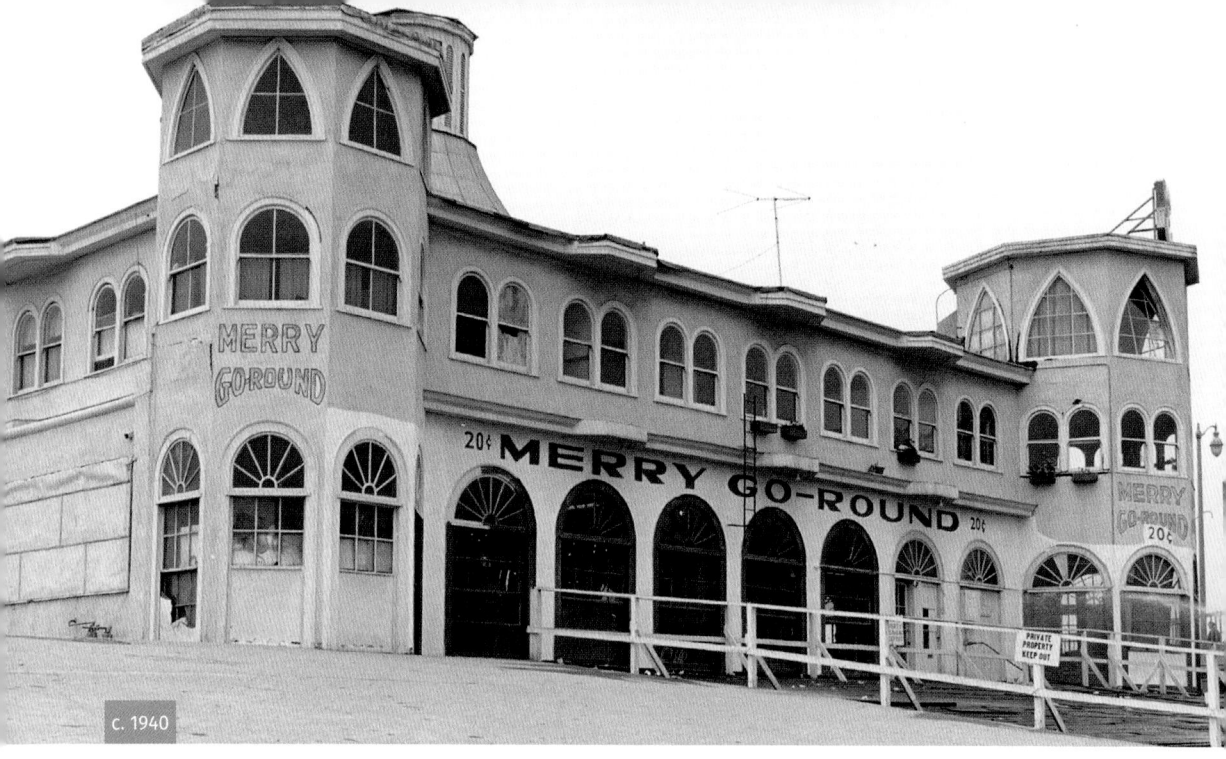

c. 1940

SANTA MONICA PIER

Still a popular destination for show-goers, anglers, and thrill-seekers

ABOVE: The first Santa Monica pier was built in 1874 at Shoo-Fly Landing, as a loading point for tar from La Brea Tar Pits. It was removed in 1879, and the current Santa Monica Pier was later built to the north. Originally two adjoining piers, the longer 1909 Municipal Pier (to carry sewage out to sea) and the shorter 1916 Looff Pleasure Pier, were strictly for entertainment and anglers. With frequent storm damage and endless renovations, the two were consolidated as the Santa Monica Pier. In 1922, on the Pleasure Pier side, a merry-go-round was installed; it became a classic. The forty-four wooden horses the children rode were hand-carved by a New York furniture maker, Charles Looff, the pier's owner. The iconic carousel was housed in the Byzantine-styled hippodrome Looff had built in 1916.

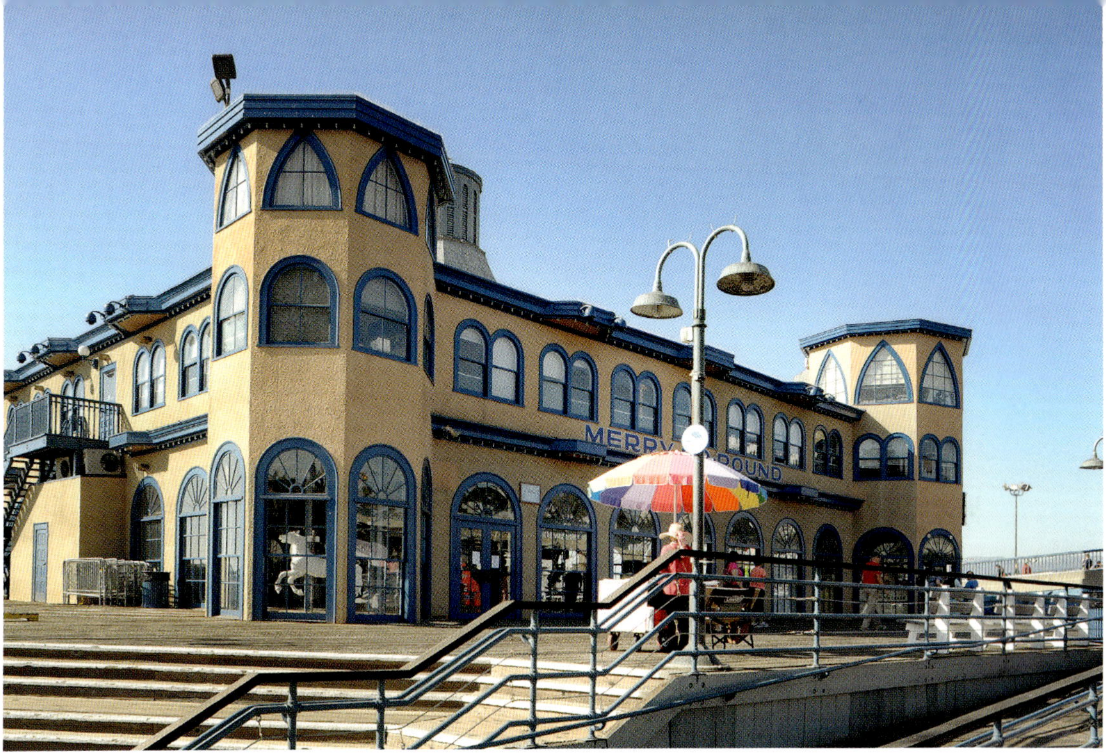

ABOVE: By the late 1960s, many attractions had gone; the Santa Monica Pier was in trouble. Listed on the National Register of Historic Places, the pier and the carousel became famous when featured in movies such as *The Sting* with Robert Redford and Paul Newman. When the Santa Monica Pier fell into disrepair in the 1970s, the carousel was threatened with destruction. But many people with fond memories fought to preserve it. In 1983 terrible rainstorms washed away part of the pier. Now the pier has been rebuilt and is heavily visited once more. The restored 1917 Billiard's Building is now home to Rusty's Surf Ranch, with vintage surfing memorabilia and billiards tournaments. Tony Award winner Paul Sand runs the new West End Theatre above the Mariasol restaurant. Le Cirque du Soleil's big top is set up each year in their trademark blue-and-yellow tents, seating 2,600 people, next to the pier. However, the Twilight Concert series in the summer has become so successful that the local council wants to scale them down because of public safety issues. The Santa Monica Pier Aquarium is below the eastern deck. The adjoining Pacific Amusement Park, which opened in 1996, has the world's first solar-powered Ferris wheel. And there's always fishing at the end of the pier.

ALSO AVAILABLE **400-page Then and Nows**

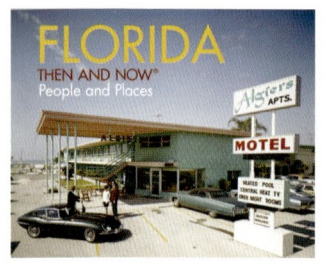

ISBN 9781909108653

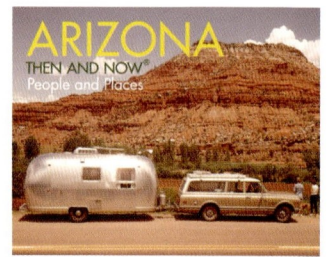

ISBN 9781909108660

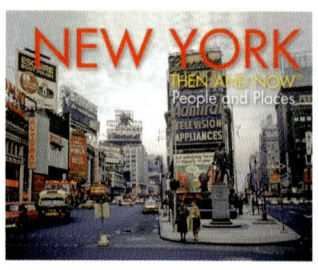

ISBN 9781862059955

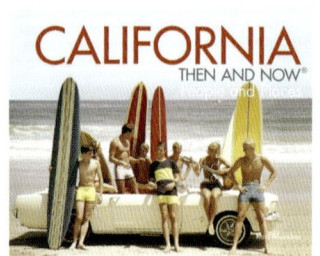

ISBN 9781862059948

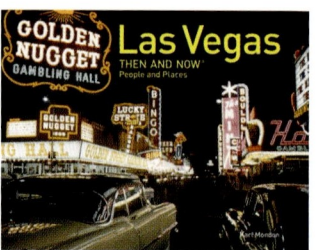

ISBN 9781911595144

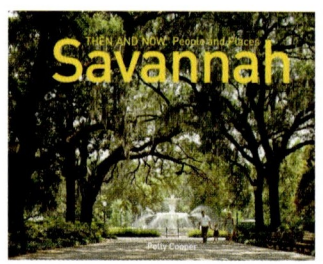

ISBN 9781910904817